The Encyclopedia of Immaturity™

VOLUME 2

by the editors of

KLUTZ®

KLUTZ®

creates activity books and other great stuff for kids ages 3 to 103. We began our corporate life in 1977 in a garage we shared with a Chevrolet Impala. Although we've outgrown that first office, Klutz galactic headquarters remains in Palo Alto, California, and we're still staffed entirely by real human beings. For those of you who collect mission statements, here's ours:

• Create wonderful things • Be good • Have fun

Write Us
We would love to hear your comments regarding this or any of our books. We have many!

KLUTZ®
450 Lambert Avenue
Palo Alto, CA 94306
USA
Book manufactured in Taiwan.

©2009 Klutz. All rights reserved. Published by Klutz, a subsidiary of Scholastic Inc. Scholastic and associated logos are trademarks and/or registered trademarks of Scholastic Inc. Klutz and associated logos are trademarks and/or registered trademarks of Klutz.

No part of this publication may be reproduced in any form or by any means without written permission of Klutz.

Distributed in the UK by Scholastic UK Ltd Westfield Road, Southam, Warwickshire England CV47 0RA

Distributed in Australia by Scholastic Australia Customer Service, PO Box 579, Gosford, NSW Australia 2250

ISBN-10: 1-59174-689-2
ISBN-13: 978-1-59174-689-8

4 1 5 8 5 7 0 8 8 8

Visit Our Website
You can check out all the stuff we make, find a nearby retailer, request a catalog, sign up for a newsletter, e-mail us, or just goof off!

www.klutz.com

Volume 1 of The Encyclopedia of Immaturity™ is available at fine retailers everywhere, as well as online.

Introduction

Growing up is a very big decision and not one that you should rush into without at least pausing for a moment to consider the implications.

Here at Klutz, for example, we've been pausing for many years. Some days, in fact, we look in our mirror and get the feeling that it might finally be time to grow up. But then we lay down, fake a burp, and the feeling passes.

Having spent a lifetime like this, we have learned a great many skills in this area, the "immaturity" area, and this volume you are holding in your hands contains many of them. Although getting older seems to be hard-wired into human beings, growing up is a choice. You can be immature, as we say, forever. You just have to be knowledgeable.

With that as your guide, we release you to browse through the rest of this volume. Please note that it is the second volume. The first volume is similar except it's red and contains more of the same, just different. Its best-selling popularity, by the way, is what inspired this work. Many of its readers have written to us saying things like "I used to act my age. But now, thanks to what I've learned from you, that's no longer my problem."

We are, of course, deeply gratified by this and hope that you too will learn how to shinny up a tree, bark like a dog, or just fake a nasty sneeze. With knowledge like that as your defense, you should be able to keep the dark forces of maturity at bay.

It's always worked for us.

John Cassidy
Palo Alto, CA

Table of Contents

*High impact
Halloween costume*

The One-Person Piggy Back

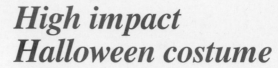

Why do some kids get a whole shovelful of candy at the same houses where all you get is a piece of fruit?

In a word, costume-impact. When all you wear is a bag over your head and a sign that says "I'm an alien. Give me candy," you're going to get a lot of apples. Sorry.

How can you change this picture? Wear the One-Person Piggy Back, a screaming hi-impact send-them-running-for-the-camera costume.

What you need:
Pair of shorts
Baseball cap
Sweatshirt
Pair of shoes
Belt
Newspaper
Lunch bag

1 Pull the shorts on, but not all the way, just to your knees. Pin them in place and leave the zipper open so you don't trip. The cuffs should hit the ground. Now put on a BIG sweatshirt and pull it all the way down to your waist.

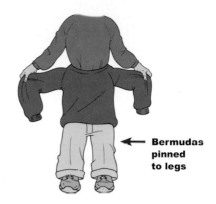

← Bermudas pinned to legs

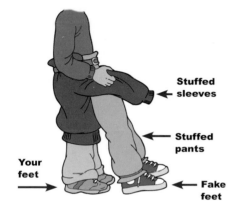

Stuffed sleeves →

Stuffed pants →

Your feet →

← Fake feet

2 With crumpled newspaper, stuff the sleeves of the sweatshirt and legs of the spare pants. Then belt the pants on as shown. Pin your spare tennis shoes to the cuffs of your pants (otherwise known as your fake legs).

3 Now pull the shoes up as shown and pin them in place. Then put the stuffed sleeves of your sweatshirt into place as shown and pin.

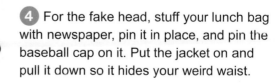

4 For the fake head, stuff your lunch bag with newspaper, pin it in place, and pin the baseball cap on it. Put the jacket on and pull it down so it hides your weird waist.

5 Now stumble around the house going "Whoooooooooooooa!"

10-minute coin magic

Be Amazing and Still Be Lazy

Great coin magic almost always requires a lot of practice and dedication. Notice we said "almost."

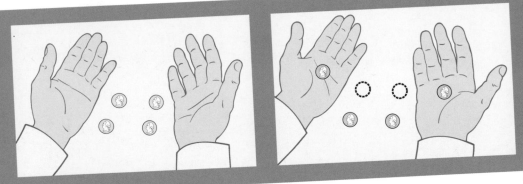

1 Start like this. Four quarters, two hands.

2 Put a quarter in each hand.

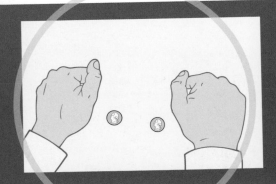

5 ...like this.

Please do what you did before. Put the coins on top of my hands.

6 Now you have to start over.

This is where the trick is done. See page 11 for the reveal.

This little bit takes a few minutes to learn — about the same as rubbing your tummy and patting your head. But the effect is slick. If you only learn one coin trick… it ought to be this one.

P.S. The real secret to great magic is presentation. Make this into a big deal with a lot of build-up.

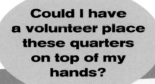

3 Close your hands and get a volunteer.

4 After your volunteer does what you've asked, then dump them back on the table…

7 Once your volunteer puts the coins back on top…

8 …"swallow" them. In other words, just open your hands quickly. And close them.

Ta-da!

9 Now make a big deal before you open your hands to reveal that there are **THREE** in one hand and **ONE** in the other. This looks like the finale, but wait… there's more!

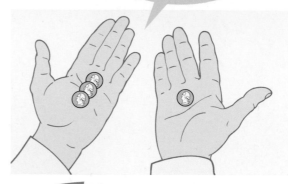

WhaAAP!!

10 Slap your hands back on the table.

FINALE

11 Uncover. **Four** under one. **None** under the other.

Unbelievable!

The secret to this is to fling the single coin across the space between the hands. Do it fast. No one will see a thing.

THE SECRET:

Go back and look at step 5. It looks like a coin from each hand is dumped back on the table. In reality, both coins come from one hand. The other hand swallows the top coin and ends up holding two.

LEFT HAND
This is the hand that dumps both of its coins.

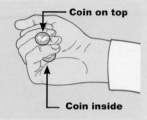

Coin on top

Coin inside

Fist is held loosely, so…

…that when you turn it over the inside coin slips out invisibly.

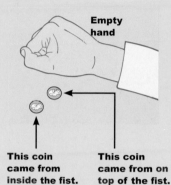

Empty hand

This coin came from inside the fist.

This coin came from on top of the fist.

RIGHT HAND
This is the hand that keeps both of its coins.

Rotate your hand to hide the trick.

① When you turn this hand over…

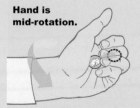

Hand is mid-rotation.

② …open your fingers so the top coin slips inside.

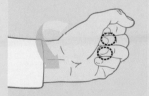

③ Close your hand in the middle of the turn.

④ Two coins inside. Nobody saw a thing.

How to disturb the peace

Make a Leaf Popper

The next time you're outside someplace where it's very quiet and calming and annoying like that, here's a great way to make a big loud noise using only natural, organic ingredients.

Find a big leaf, the size of your palm. If it's thick and waxy, it makes a louder noise.

1 Make a loose fist as shown and cover the hole with the leaf.

2 Hold your other hand flat, palm down, and bring it down hard onto the leaf.

Repeat with new leaf.

**Dry, brittle don't work.
Green, thin do.**

BANG!

Every Party's Got a Squirter

You're at an adult party where everyone is standing around with a wineglass in their hand and talking. And that's it; nothing else is happening.

Is this a nightmare situation? Yes.

Can you do something about it? Yes.

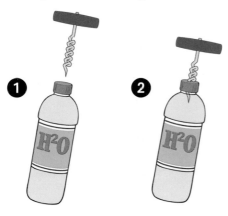

❶ **❷** **❸**

There will be small bottles of fancy water in the drink tub. Go get one.

There will be a corkscrew somewhere near the wine. Go get it.

Twist a little hole in the lid of the water bottle. You now have a loaded water weapon. All you need to do is squeeze.

Why not shake up the bubbly water bottles while you're over by the drink tub? And then put them back. It doesn't take but a moment, and it'll make the party more fun to watch when random people open them up.

The last time your friend will ever fall asleep at your house

So That's Who You're Dreaming About

The next time you're at a sleepover and your friend has fallen asleep, draw a thought balloon on a piece of paper with some boy's name on it and a bunch of hearts. Then hold it over her head and snap a cell phone shot.

Select all your friends and push "send."

Simple? Yes. But, it's the simple gestures that often mean the most.

Make a Juice Box Straw Rocket

By stomping on an empty milk carton that you've re-closed, you can make a pretty good bang. (If you don't already know this, there's nothing we can do for you.)

But it's a different story with juice boxes. Because of the straw hole, all they do is pffffft when you stomp. Frustrating.

What to do?

Tie a knot in the straw and stick it back in (after you've finished the drink). Then stomp on it. The straw will go rocketing off. Watch you don't put an eye out.

Key point: knot the straw.

And how weird is your friend?

How Weird Are You?

Many people think that just because they can bend their thumb back at a weird angle, that makes them extraordinary beings. Well, guess what, people. Everybody can bend their thumb back at a weird angle. We've done the research. Plus, (almost) everybody can curl their tongue into a tube, too. So there.

Frankly, these kinds of shallow claims have been very frustrating to those of us who are, in fact, truly weird.

In an effort to get past the poseurs, and to establish a *Universal Measure of Weirdness* (The Klutz Weirdness Factor, or KWF) that all of us can agree upon, we have created here a set of ten questions. You and your friends should answer all of them — and be prepared to demonstrate — in order to finally establish a standard measure.

Our dream is that, over time, all citizens will know their KWF and be expected to provide it on job and school applications.

1 Make Darth Vader breathing sounds with cupped hands.
❏ Can   ❏ Cannot

2 Shake hands with self behind back, one hand over shoulder.
❏ Can   ❏ Cannot

3 Fish lips (must wiggle them).
❏ Can   ❏ Cannot

4 Form tip of tongue into "W."
❏ Can   ❏ Cannot

5 Crack knuckles.
❏ Can   ❏ Cannot

6 Touch elbow with tongue.
❏ Can   ❏ Cannot

7 Flip eyelids back.
❏ Can   ❏ Cannot

8 Roll upper lip back, stick to upper gums, so that front teeth are exposed, beaver-style.
❏ Can   ❏ Cannot

9 Gleeking (look it up).
❏ Can   ❏ Cannot

10 Burp at will.
❏ Can   ❏ Cannot

In order to get your KWF, simply add up all the "Can's." One point each.

Show Us Your Proboscis

Each of these words is a body part. This kid has all 10. So do you. The question is, where are they? Connect the dots.

Proboscis ●

Epiglottis ●

Umbilicus ●

Philtrum ●

Hallux ●

Wemus ●

Hippocampus ●

Humerus ●

Cowlick ●

Intertragic notch ●

See page 197 for answers.

How to Get Flushed Away

Stand up on a toilet seat (you need to be in a middle school bathroom first). Look over the stall wall and tell all the other kids, "Hey!!! Check this out!" Then with your foot hit the flush lever and as it flushes, scream and drop down out of sight.

Why wait for nature?

How to Make Rude Noises Three Ways

Over the years, we have been frequently surprised and disappointed to discover how many fine students are unable to make rude noises except by accident. Frankly, it's upsetting. What kind of a world do we live in where young people — the future of our nation! — cannot make a farting noise whenever they choose?

Here are the instructions. Learn them and go forth.

TECHNIQUE NUMBER 1

Form a pocket between your hands.

Squeeze all the air out, and make a tight seal.

Separate your hands. Break the seal, and make that suction cup kind of noise.

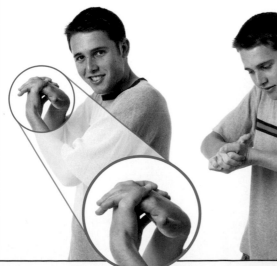

BLaT!

TECHNIQUE NUMBER 2

By blowing hard into your elbow like this, you can make a lovely noise that's very similar sounding to…

…TECHNIQUE NUMBER 3

Some people think this one sounds a little wetter, but it's a matter of personal taste.

Teachers hate this one
Pencil Battles

Let's make you **Player A** and the other guy **Player B**.

Player B (the other guy) is holding a pencil as shown — lying flat on top of two fingers. He's on the defense.

Player A (that would be you, on offense) is preparing to thwap **Player B**'s pencil and break it in two. Look at the photo for how to thwap. It's like a karate chop with a pencil.

The rules: Pretty simple: You try to break the other guy's pencil taking turns. Yes, there are some tricks, but you'll have to let experience be your guide.

PLAYER A
(YOU)

PLAYER B
(THE OTHER GUY)

Achoo!
How to Fake a Cold

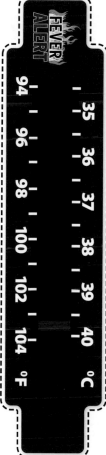

You know how parents always love to play make-believe games. Here's one they're sure to enjoy. Make it a secret and play it some school day morning.

1 Get out of bed and run in place until you're all hot and sweaty. Get back into bed.

2 Cut out this perma-fever thermometer and hold it to your forehead.

3 When necessary, sniffle, cough and ask for water… water… and maybe some of those cherry-flavored cough drops, too.

Root beer!

Send a Toiletgram™!

Make a Potty Pal

Here's an easy way to make a new friend in a faraway land. It's like they do in the movies when they put a message into a bottle and toss it into the ocean. Only better because it doesn't need any oceans.

Just write your message on a sheet of toilet paper. Don't forget your return address. That's step one.
Next, flush it away to who knows where.
Done! Now all you have to do is wait!

This way to your new friend.

With lids

How to Play Indoor Frisbee® Golf

Players stand in the kitchen, someone looks out for Mom, and the rest tee off towards the bathroom. First one to the bathroom sink (for example) is the winner. Try 9 holes and experiment to find the best course.

Fore!

WHICH LIDS FLY THE BEST?

Generally speaking, the bigger the better. Avoid Tupperware™. Too heavy.

Hand Faces

We call this first one "Get a Grip on Thumbman." The other two are called "A Tribute to Me and My Many Moods."

You'll need a skin-safe pen and a moment or two in the back of the class.

Technically,
dime-in-ring

Give Mom a Diamond Ring

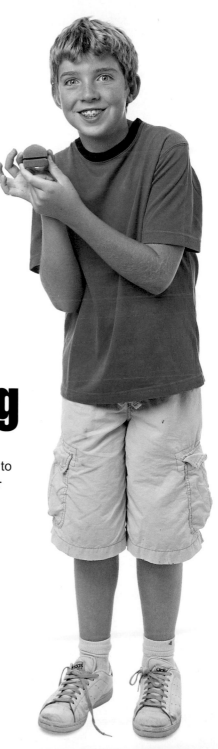

Maybe you've been trying to get down to the jewelry store recently to get your mom a huge diamond ring? But something always comes up? Homework? Chores?

We totally understand. But in the meantime, here's a ring that you can make at home. Cost? $1.10.

1 Start with a crisp new bill. Put a perfect crease lengthwise right down the middle.

Crease here.

A crease means fold and unfold.

2 Now fold at the dotted lines. Fold toward you. Make sure the edges…

Fold here.

Fold here.

THIS IS THE CREASE YOU PUT IN LAST STEP

…meet at the center crease exactly.

Your buck will look like this.

3 Make two more lengthwise creases by folding the top and bottom edges into the center.

Run your thumbnail along these folds to make them really sharp before you unfold them.

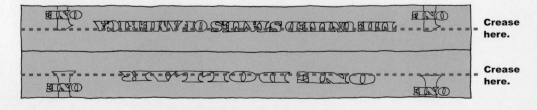

Crease here.

Crease here.

4 You'll end up looking like this. Now fold your buck in half as shown, bringing the right edge <u>back</u> to meet the left edge. Fold away from you.

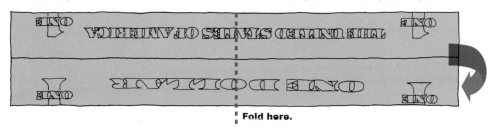

Fold here.

End up looking like this.

5 Crease on the dotted lines. Remember, to make a crease you have to fold <u>and</u> unfold.

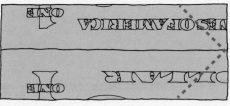

6 Now, push the two corners in so they meet <u>between</u> the two layers of the bill. If this doesn't work well, go back and make sure the folds in step 5 are really sharp.

Pushed in.

Push in.

If you've done these two "push-in-folds" right, you'll have a smooth point on the folded end of the bill.

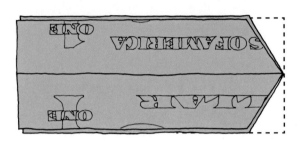

7 Look at your bill and confirm that there are two layers: the top and the bottom. In the next few steps, you'll only be working with the <u>top</u> layer. Fold <u>just the top layer</u> as shown.

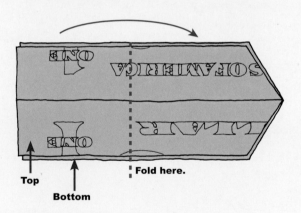

Top

Bottom

Fold here.

8 Still working with the top layer, fold on the dotted lines so the edges meet in the middle.

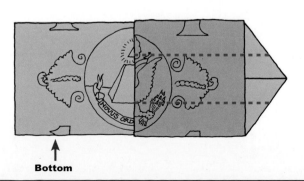

Bottom

End up like this:

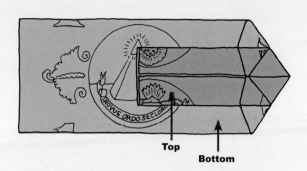

Top

Bottom

9 Now turn the bill over so you can work on the bottom layer. Fold the edges into the center...

Fold down.

Fold up.

...so you get this.

10 Turn the bill over again, and make sure it matches the illustration. If it does, take a deep breath and carry on. If not, go back a few steps to find out where you went wrong.

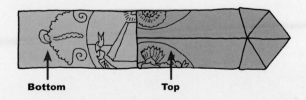

Bottom

Top

11 This next step will make the ring band and dime box. Put the buck down in front of you. Hold the bottom layer down and flip the top layer over as shown.

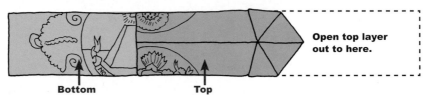

Hold bottom down.

Bottom **Top**

Open top layer out to here.

End up like this.

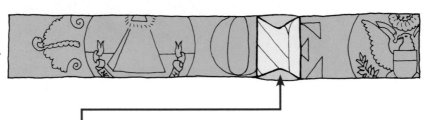

The **dime box** will look a little smooshed, so use the eraser end of a pencil or your finger to shape it into a neat square little box with a flat bottom, like so:

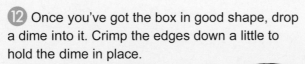

12 Once you've got the box in good shape, drop a dime into it. Crimp the edges down a little to hold the dime in place.

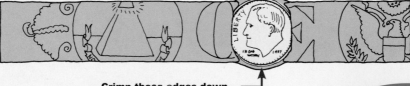

Crimp these edges down.

If you want to taper the ring band, now's the time. This is optional, but it will make the ring a little nicer.

13

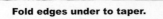

Fold edges under to taper.

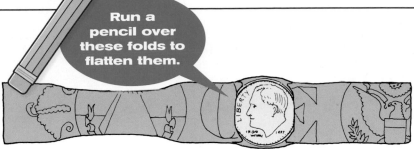

Run a pencil over these folds to flatten them.

Go ahead and cheat. Tape the ends closed.

14 Curve the buck into a ring and tuck the long end into the folds of the short end. Go ahead and cheat a little by tapering the long end so it tucks in easier.

If the ring is too big for you, fold the long end to make it shorter before you tuck it into the other end.

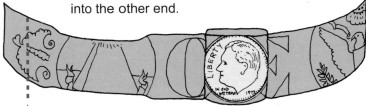

Fold here to make the ring smaller.

YOWZA!

Never take this ring apart; you'll never need a buck that badly.

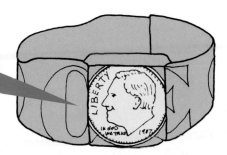

How to Bark Like a Dog

Every fourth grade class throughout the world has one kid who can fake the sound of someone vomiting really well. And another kid who can fake the sound of a barking dog. Sometimes they're even the same kid, but in all cases, they are the most important individuals in their class, role models for the rest of the students.

How to vomit (or at least sound like it) is something so special… we're going to save for the next volume of this encyclopedia. How to bark like a dog, on the other hand, has three key steps. They are as follows:

1 Cup your hands around your mouth as shown, leaving a little daylight.

2 Snort two or three times. (Snorting happens on the intake. If you do not already know how to snort, we have nothing more we can say to you. Stop reading here.) This is the preliminary growl. Very important.

Leave an opening.

3 Bark. It comes from down low, like a cough. It's not really a vocal chords thing. Ask your dog.

4 Repeat as necessary.

SCRATCH

Scratch

EXTRA CREDIT: Learn how to scratch fleas

How to Make a Fauxhawk

All you need is gel or hairspray. You can mohawk your hair, show Granny, take it down, and still stay in the will.

Look! Up in the sky!
It's a bird. It's a plane. It's…

The Oldest Trick in the Book

Wow!

?

Check it out!

Slappy Games

PANCAKES

Put both your hands out flat. The other guy puts his on top. Your job is to whip your hands out from under his and slap the tops of his hands before he can get them away. If you fake going, and he flinches, you get a free slap.

COMING FROM BEHIND

The other guy holds his hands in front as shown. You put both hands behind your back and attempt to come out fast enough to slap his. A whiff means you switch places.

PUSHOVER

Both parties stand face to face, toe to toe. Hold your hands up, palms out. The challenge is to push the other guy's hands so he falls over backwards. The danger? If you go for a shove, and he relaxes his arms, you'll push against no resistance and throw yourself off balance, making you the loser.

How to Mess Up Family Portraits

THE SELF-STRANGLE

THE HIGH WAIST

THE BARF

Are You a Genius?

How to Make the Teacher Think You're Chewing Gum

Sit at your desk in the middle of class, close your eyes and stick your feet way out while you fake the look of a cow chewing its cud. If you really want to get into it, you can snap a pencil against the desk for the "snapping gum" sfx.

When the teacher yells at you to take out your gum, act innocent and shocked — that she should even suggest such a thing! And then stick your finger in your mouth and root all around proving there's nothing there. Give her a big smile at the end.

Trust us! Teachers LOVE this one!

Great Cell Phone Shots

These shots fall into a category we call cell phone camera shenanigans. Hopefully, they're self-explanatory. The makeout fakeout is a traditional pose (requires only one person by the way). The other shots require two.

THE MAKEOUT FAKEOUT

HEIGHT OVERNIGHT

There's a stool here that you can't see.

THE TAKEOUT HEAD

THE BIG STRETCH

Basketball and Egg Launch

This one's a little controversial since an egg goes flying at the end of it. Do it outside and clear it with the relevant authorities.

Arrange the egg on top of the ball as shown.

Drop the ball straight down. The egg will sit on top until the ball hits the ground at which point the ball will pretty much stop and the egg will really take off. It's amazing. We were able to catch our egg and put it back in the fridge. But, on the other hand, we ARE professionals.

Note egg.

Be careful it doesn't hit you on the way up.

Snap Tops

It's amazing, sometimes, how small skills can lead to big social results.

Learn this little item and you will dominate the social food chain at your home, school, or workplace.

Almost any kind of plastic lid works.

1 Put the rim of the lid between two ready-to-snap fingers.

2 Elbow very high. Lid by ear.

15–20 feet, no problem

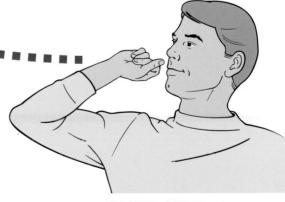

3 Snap fingers.
DON'T MOVE ARM!

Naming the New You

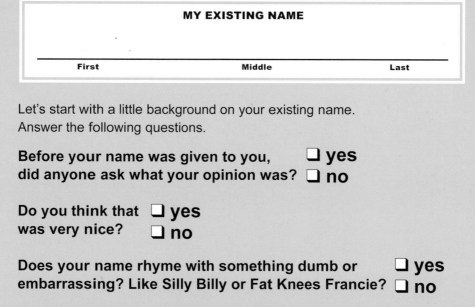

Write your existing name in the space provided below. First, middle, and last — in that order. Afterwards, check the spelling and then go on to the next step.

MY EXISTING NAME

_____

First   Middle   Last

Let's start with a little background on your existing name. Answer the following questions.

Before your name was given to you, did anyone ask what your opinion was? ❏ yes ❏ no

Do you think that was very nice? ❏ yes ❏ no

Does your name rhyme with something dumb or embarrassing? Like Silly Billy or Fat Knees Francie? ❏ yes ❏ no

Should this have been easily foreseen by any semi-aware person? ❏ yes ❏ no

After doing this exercise you may realize that you've been saddled with a name that just doesn't work for the new you. This is what happens when well-meaning people start getting into your business. It's like when parents tell you what to wear. Only it's permanent.

What to do? Changing your whole name is a problem — filling out all the forms and explaining to all your friends and so forth. We suggest you keep the basics but modify it. As follows:

- If you're going to grow up to be a spoiled rock star, try one of your pet's names along with the street you live on — or lived on. For example, I (John Cassidy) turn into Bright Eyes Timberwood.

- If you're going to grow up to be a real estate mogul, just put "The" in front of your first name. Example: Karen Phillips = The Karen.

- If you're going to grow up to become an alien, just jumble all the letters of your first name to make your new alien name, and your last name (all jumbled) becomes your home planet. Example: George Tubble becomes "Eegrog from the planet Blubte."

- If you're going to grow up to be a movie star just cup your hands around your mouth and try saying this in a deep voice: "Starrrrrinnnnngggg (YOUR NAME HERE)!!!!!." If it sounds ridiculous try to grow up and be something else.

- If you're going to grow up to become a caveman, just use the first sound of your last name and then put a lot of "uggh's" or "oggh's" in. Example: Jason becomes Jasoggh.

- If you're going to grow up to be a trapeze artist, put "ini" after your last name and put the words "The Amazing" in front of it. Example: Ishmael Puttuck becomes The Amazing Puttuckini.

- If you're going to grow up to be a new breakfast cereal, just put the word "New Toasted" in front of your last name, and "Flakes" behind it. Example: Roxanne Scorbunt becomes New Toasted Scorbunt Flakes.

- If you're going to grow up to be a pirate, just replace your first name with "Blood-'n'-guts." For example, Orson Peanuckle becomes "Blood-'n'-guts" Peanuckle.

Watch very carefully.

How to Freeze Shoelace Atoms

Hold a shoelace (or any string) tightly as shown and launch into some version of the following speech:

> *Please do not talk or ask questions during this demonstration. It depends on a complete absence of moving air currents. Even a single breath can disturb the atoms and the entire process.*
>
> *As you can see, I am holding this shoelace in a vertical orientation. If you will please touch the shoelace — gently — you will sense that it is warm, approximately room temperature (let them touch it).*
>
> *Warm, isn't it? Those of you who have studied quantum physics will understand what that means — all the shoelace atoms are racing around at super high speed. But watch! I will blow on the string… (do that for a while)… and then I will remove my hand and the string will remain vertical!! Frozen stiff!! (Don't do anything for a second.) You don't believe me do you? Watch…!*

…then, remove your lower hand.

I will take my hand off of this string, and yet it will remain…

…VERTICAL.

Summertime snowballs

How to Make and Throw a Sloshie

Take a few sheets of toilet paper, soak in water, throw. Any questions?

1

You will need toilet paper, a few sheets, and water.

2

Soak toilet paper.

3 Throw.

And "Good Work" stickers

Book Covers

Cut out the book cover opposite this page (or photocopy it if this is someone else's book) and use it to cover any book whose cover might arouse unwanted interest. Protects both the book AND you!

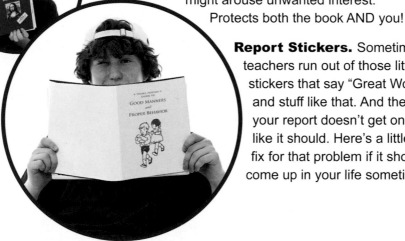

Before

Report Stickers. Sometimes teachers run out of those little stickers that say "Great Work" and stuff like that. And then your report doesn't get one like it should. Here's a little fix for that problem if it should come up in your life sometime.

Before

After

A YOUNG PERSON'S GUIDE TO

GOOD MANNERS
and
PROPER BEHAVIOR

World's Funniest Joke

A professor in England (Dr. Richard Wiseman) ran an on-line joke contest for a year, receiving more than 14,000 jokes and running them by sample groups throughout the world.

The winner never got the top spot in any single country, but it did the best on average. Personally, we don't think it's all that super, but read it and see what you think.

Two hunters are out in the woods when one of them collapses. He doesn't seem to be breathing and his eyes are glazed. The other guy whips out his phone and calls the emergency services. He gasps, "My friend is dead! What can I do?" The operator says, "Calm down. I can help. First, let's make sure he's dead." There is a silence, then a shot is heard. Back on the phone, the guy says, "OK, now what?"

WORLD'S FURTHEST JOKE

Alan Shepard, in 1971, snuck a golf club and golf ball onboard Apollo 14 and hit a drive which has been described as the longest ever hit since it disappeared out of view. **Honorable Mention:** Astronaut Clay Anderson spent six months on the International Space Station. Toward the end of his tour, fighting boredom, he radioed down to Mission Control. "What's the difference between roast beef and pea soup?" Mission Control had no idea. Clayton responded, "Anybody can roast beef."

WORLD'S LAMEST JOKE

WORLD'S OLDEST JOKE

Reproduced below is a hieroglyph located on an Egyptian tomb. Date: 1400 B.C. **The setup:** A servant is sleeping in a wine storage room. A man is knocking at the door with a wine jar to store. Behind him is a progression of men bringing more wine. No one is answering. The man knocking says to the man behind him, "The servant is asleep." **Here comes the punch line:** The funny guy, the guy with the jar on his head, quips: "He is drunk from wine," while the servant behind the door calls out, "I haven't slept a wink." (Hey! We didn't say it's the funniest joke. Just the oldest.)

Reproduction of wall painting from the tomb of Intef. Thebes, 18th Dynasty.

Funny guy

The guy knocking

The servant. The butt of the joke

MOST DANGEROUS JOKE

Any joke — when you're in church, class, or a museum — can be deadly.

THIS KID IS DOOMED.

Scientists call it "church laughter" and you know the drill. You're at a deadly silent religious service, surrounded by old ladies wearing stern looks, when you look up and some "friend" makes a funny face at you. You snicker and the women look at you. Not good. So you cover your mouth which, of course, makes you gag. This is the tipping point. Because a kid in church with his hand stuck in his mouth trying not to laugh is a very funny picture. If you register that, and start laughing even harder — you get into a feedback loop and you're doomed.

In January of 1962 probably the worst outbreak ever recorded took place in the East African town of Kanshasa when three schoolgirls lost it in class and spread a "laughter epidemic" that did not peter out for six months "forcing the closure of 14 schools and affecting approximately 1,000 people in tribes bordering Lake Victoria in Tanganyika and Uganda." (Hey! Google it if you don't believe us. *Tanganyika laughter epidemic.*)

AMERICAN SIGN LANGUAGE JOKE

A squeezing hand is ASL for milk. If you pass that sign in front of your eyes, that translates as Passed Your Eyes Milk. Get it? Say it out loud.

THE WORLD'S ONLY FUNNY MATHEMATICAL JOKE

There are only three kinds of people in this world.

Those who can count...

...and those who can't.

THE ONLY JOKE THAT CHIMPS GET

It has been known since Darwin's time that chimpanzees can and do laugh. However, they apparently only get one joke, the mock chase which you'll remember as the bit where your parents fake like they're monsters and stomp around chasing you, saying "Here I cooooooooome!" Apparently chimps do it to each other a lot and it kills them everytime.

WORLD'S SMARTEST JOKE

Isaac Newton (1642–1727) is often described as one of the smartest men who ever lived. He was not, however, the life of the party. His longtime assistant testified that he could think of only one occasion upon which his boss had ever laughed. According to the story, the famous scientist was in a room once and overheard someone say: "What is the value of studying geometry?" Hahahahahaha!

Your House, the Jungle Gym

Have you ever wondered what you'd do if your hallway were covered in hot lava? Don't you think a little practice and planning now, when it's safe, makes a lot more sense than later, after some volcano goes off and there's no time to "figure it out?"

What follow are simple steps for climbing down a hallway without touching the floor. By the way, if anyone comes by and asks, you're conducting a "hot lava in the hallway safety drill."

HALLWAY CLIMBING TWO WAYS

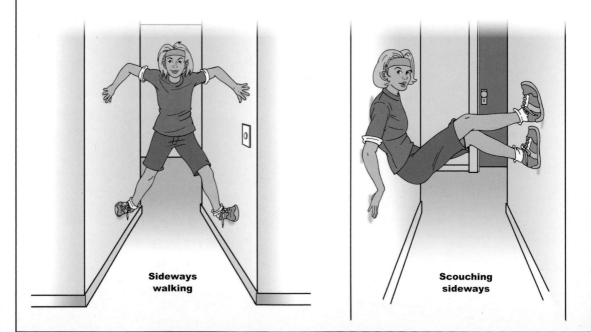

Sideways walking

Scouching sideways

DOORNASTICS

Doorway chin-ups

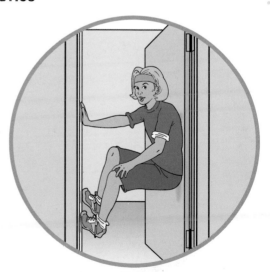

Doorway climbing

And other sleepover gymnastics

How to Stand on Your Hands

These activities fall into a category we call "sleepover gymnastics," the kind of thing you might do in front of a rented movie or while you're waiting for the pizza. The simplest one here is The Human Chair. The other two are pretty tough but in a good-sized sleepover usually somebody can do at least one of them.

EXERCISE 1:
THE HANDSTAND

DIFFICULTY
FACTOR

MEDIUM

EXERCISE 2:
THE HUMAN CHAIR

DIFFICULTY FACTOR
EASY

EXERCISE 3:
THE HUMAN SEESAW

DIFFICULTY FACTOR
HARD

Let your rear hang way out like this, not on her knees.

Grab her with your feet around the waist. If you get your feet into her armpits, it won't work.

EXERCISE 4:
HOW TO FALL THROUGH THE FLOOR

This is one of those brain/body illusions. Let's make you the kid lying down. Your friend pulls your arms up while you close your eyes and relax and think deep thoughts. After a while of being stretched, your friend should s…l…o…w…ly let you back down to the ground. It will feel as if the floor has sunk and you are being let down into a hole.

HOW TO BODY SURF
The bottom kids are the logs. They all roll at once.

EXERCISE 5:
THE WEIRD ARM MUNCHKIN

There probably isn't a single summer camp in the entire world that doesn't do this routine. We'll make you the front kid and your friend the back kid. You should kneel in your shoes and your friend needs to snuggle up behind you and stick their hands through the big sweatshirt you've worn for the occasion. Your own hands you should tuck out of the way inside your sweatshirt. It depends on the summer camp, but usually what happens next is the back kid washes the face of the front kid, then brushes her teeth, and then tries to serve her cereal. It usually makes a huge mess and always brings down the house.

EXERCISE 6:
THE TREE

EXERCISE 7:
THE GROUP SIT

EXERCISE 8:
THE LOTUS POSITION

64

EXERCISE 9:

In our group only one girl out of 15 could make this work. Don't get stuck.

EXERCISE 10:
WONDER WOMAN

The big secret: Bend your knees and drop your butt way low before you pull your superhero onto your back.

THE BACK-TO-BACK VARIATION

Tin Can Telephone

There's a category of toys and skills that everyone (especially parents) remembers fondly from ye olde tymes when life was simpler and far better. Things like secret ink you can make from lemon juice, or kites you can make from newspaper, or bottle rockets, or dandelion tea, etc., etc.

Here's the standard line: "Why do you need video games? Granddad used to play with all these simple toys, back before TV and all that."

Well, all we can say is, if he did, he must have been a very frustrated guy with a finger or two probably missing. Because lemon juice ink that shows up on a letter when you heat it just doesn't work. Nor does a newspaper kite. A bottle rocket using black powder is both illegal and incredibly dangerous (although exciting, we'll confess), and dandelion tea tastes exactly like hot, bitter water.

Punch a hole in the bottom of the can and knot the string through it.

We'll admit another thing: Tin can telephones actually do work. We were dubious, too, but we made a pair and they work even if you just whisper. Keep the line tight. Who knew?

PILL BUG BINGO

13	25	43	51	69
9	21	38	59	62
5	29	FREE SPOT	49	64
11	26	45	57	66
6	19	39	52	70

CAN YOU GUESS WHAT THIS IS A REAL PHOTO OF?

In Texas, and places like that, a popular fund-raising activity is called Cow Pie Bingo. Schools are particularly fond of it. A football field is gridded out like a huge bingo card and all the squares are sold to bettors for a few dollars each. Next, a farmer is found who will lend out a well-fed cow for the big night when the stands are filled in anticipation. (Can you see where this is going?) The cow is released onto the field and if he (or she) deposits on your square, you're a WINNER! Collect 10x your investment. The school takes the rest.

Great idea! But what about the rest of us? That don't have a cow, a farmer, or a football field? Not a problem.

Go outside and find a pill bug. Then, after you've sold all the squares on this grid, set him down on it and let him wander about until… BINGO!

By the way, pill bugs make great bingo players since their poop is cubicle so it won't roll around. (Look it up if you don't believe us.)

*Cannonballs
vs. can openers*

How to Get
People Wet

Whenever we have a scientific question, we always ask our favorite scientist, Paul Doherty of the San Francisco Exploratorium. The reason is because he always knows the answer. For example, if the question is, How do you make the biggest possible splash off the diving board? The answer is: Get into the can opener position, spring as high as you can, and hit the water at 35 degrees. If you have a target, point your feet towards it.

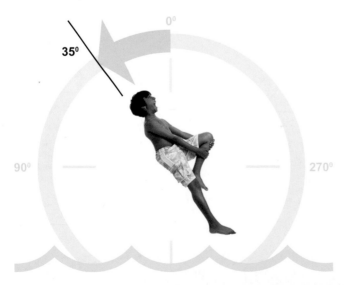

0⁰

35⁰

90⁰   270⁰

THE BEST ANGLE
TO HIT THE WATER

Enter the water at 35 degrees from vertical. Then, as your butt hits the water, lean back by pulling your leg up so the body plunges into the water more nearly horizontal.

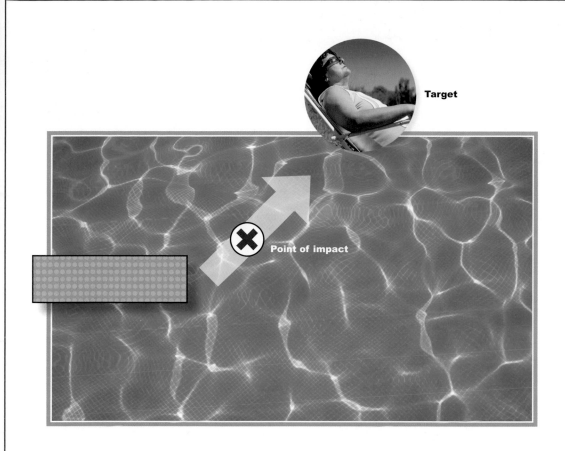

Target

Point of impact

THE PHYSICS OF THE CANNONBALL

Some kids favor the cannonball, but they have been misinformed. Paul says: "The size of the splash depends on how big and how fast you can put a hole in the water. A cannonball leaves a smaller-sized hole than a can opener. It's not the worst splash-making dive (that would be a plain old regular dive). But it's no can opener."

How to Be the Fourth Stooge

It's natural to have dreams — even big dreams — and you would be dishonest to yourself if you didn't try to pursue yours. "Go for it!" That's our advice. "Don't worry what other people might say! Chase your dreams!"

For example, let's say your dream is to be the fourth stooge, but you don't want someone always poking your eyes out. No problem, just put your hand up (see illus) and block! Key point: Don't take it away when the other guy says "Count your fingers!" Ignore him, or count your other hand.

And what about hair pulling? Won't that hurt?

Not if you do it our way:

Make a fist and hold it firmly against your head. The other guy grabs it and pulls. Meanwhile, you try to keep it planted to your head and make a bunch of weird painful faces as he "drags" you around.

The same thing works for nose twisting.

The other guy makes a fist (as shown) and plants it up against your nose as you grab him by the wrist. (By the way, he doesn't actually grab your nose, it just looks that way.) Then he twists and you get to make painful noises and twist your head in the right direction as he "drags" you around.

Nyuk, nyuk, nyuk.

Sibling abuse

How to Make Your Little Brother a Super Hero

72

Payback

How to Help Your Sister

Are you always looking for little ways to help your little sister with her little problems? Like when her dessert is too big for her to eat all by herself? Things like that?

Of course you are.

Now imagine how bad you'd feel if she ever got locked out of her dumb diary because she lost the little tiny key? How can you help? Even when she's not there?

1 Get a bobby pin and stick it into the lock as shown.

2 Twist and fool around until it opens. The locks are so lame this almost always works.

The universal homework excuse

A Note from Your Dog

Here's a note to give to your teacher whenever this common misfortune befalls you. Just copy and fill in the blanks.

"Dear Ms. _____, My name is Biskut and I em _____'s dog. I don't no of eny gud way to say this, so I'm just going 2 say it: Last nite I had an akcident on _____'s homewurk. It's unfortunet, but it happpened and I take fullll responsibilitee four it. I apologiz. I have a medical condition and thingz happen unexpektedly now. Sorry.

Signed,

(P.S. By the way, I got a quik glance at it befor the incident and it lookked like excelllent wurk. Just thot you'd like to know.)

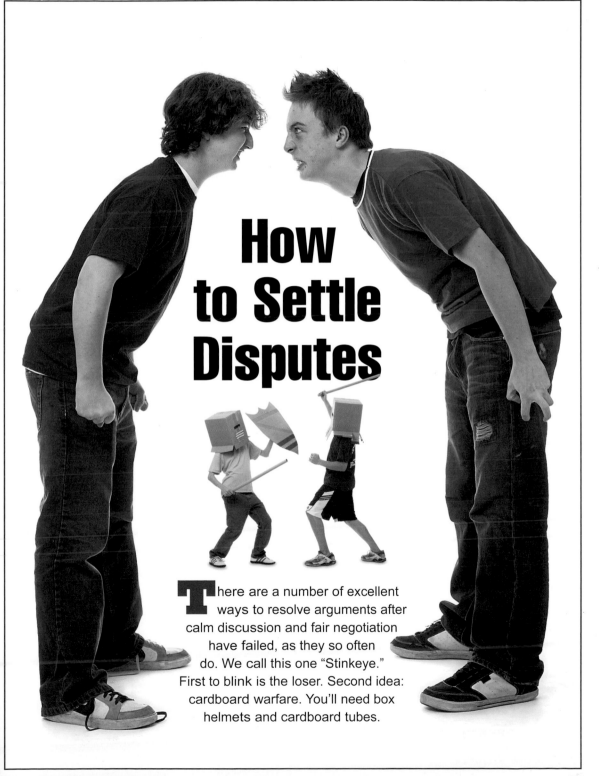

How to Settle Disputes

There are a number of excellent ways to resolve arguments after calm discussion and fair negotiation have failed, as they so often do. We call this one "Stinkeye." First to blink is the loser. Second idea: cardboard warfare. You'll need box helmets and cardboard tubes.

The Raisin Box Kazoo

1 Eat raisins.

2 Stick empty box in mouth.

3 Blow.

HOW TO PLAY THE BOTTLE

If you don't have a bottle handy, the caps to some big fat markers can work, too.

Tweet!

For when you forget that pooper scooper

Doggie Doo Cover

Photocopy a stack of these to use if you're out walking the dog and you need to cover up an unexpected incident. Try to use them only in emergencies since the effect is only short-term.

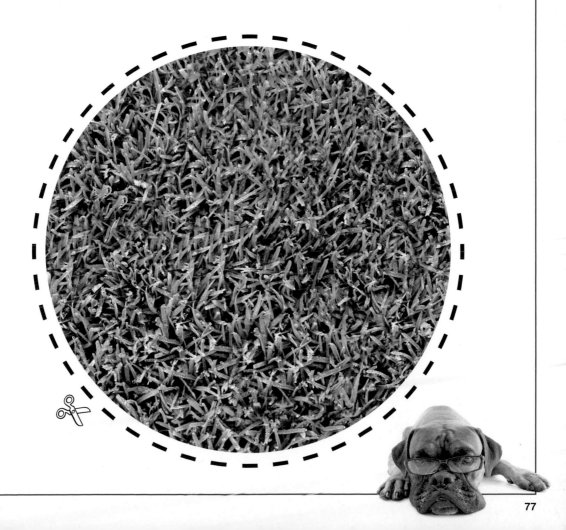

Plate Covers

Do you ever get the old "Clean your plate or no dessert for you!" business? How annoying is that? Especially when it's liver and onions night.

Fake plate →
Food →
Real plate →

Fortunately, we have a solution, our Clean Plate Cover Ups. Photocopy this page at 200% and cut on the dotted line. Then slap one of them right on top of the nasty vegetables when you get an opening. Next, before anyone gets a good look, head for the sink to wash up. Keep talking, walk quickly, scrape that plate, and you should be golden.

Let me just take this plate to the sink, mom.

Photocopy size up 200% and then cut on dotted line.

Psycho Tickling

Slowly, verrrry sloooooowly, bring your finger to a point right between the eyes of whoever's right in front of you. DON'T TOUCH! But leave your fingertip half-a-millimeter away from their quivering flesh. They will experience a strange, very irritating, tingle at the point you're almost touching.

Dog Couture

We used to think that accessories were the only thing that separated us from the lower animals. But that was before we started putting glasses and hats on our dogs and taking pictures. Now we're not so sure. Big Hint: We used tape to hold the glasses on and little doggie treats so our models would sit still for their photos.

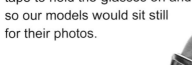

Air Guitar

Playing air guitar is just like regular guitar only without the strings. Or guitar. You just need to get a lot of body energy into it.

The world championships, incidentally, are held every year in Europe where the contestants train like crazy (check out Air Guitar Nation for a great documentary on the subject). We recommend training to "Purple Haze" or "Stairway to Heaven."

Five Facts You Need to Know Before You Turn the Next Page

1 **Possibly the most unbelievable fact of all time.** A guy in France used to perform on stage with an act built around his amazing ability to control his farting. His stage name was Le Petomane and he was huge in the 1890s. He could play recognizable tunes, imitate thunder, and put out a candle at 10 feet. For a time, he was the star attraction at the Moulin Rouge where he played to packed houses.

Le Petomane

In one incident, a woman in the audience became so overcome with hysterics that she fell out of her seat "and had to be carried out of the theatre by ushers for her own safety." Towards the end of his career, he would climax his act by performing his own version of the San Francisco Earthquake of 1906. His real name, by the way, was Joseph Pujol (1857–1945) and the science behind his act… lay in his unique ability to control his abdominal muscles.

2 **Possibly the second most unbelievable fact of all time.** Another guy, also French, adopted the stage name Mssr. Mange Tout (Mr. Eat Anything). He has eaten, at one time or another, a TV, a large number of grocery carts, a bicycle, and, in his grandest gesture, a small airplane (Cessna 150). He is, according to Dr. Bernan Morzol who has studied him for many years, 'basically… a normal guy" except he has an extra thick stomach lining and extraordinary enzymes.

His real name, by the way, is Michel Lotito and, according to his wife, he also eats regular food as well.

❸ And you thought winning the lottery took luck.

During WWII, a guy jumped out of his airplane when it broke apart in mid-air over France. As unfortunate as this sounds, it gets worse. He wasn't wearing a parachute and he was more than 3 miles above the ground.

Obviously, his future was not bright, and the fact that he was hurtling towards a stone railway station would not, at first glance, seem to offer much consolation. But the station had a skylight which he managed to crash through. Somehow, the breaking glass slowed him enough so that he was not only able to survive the fall, he came back to the station some 50 years later for a celebration the French villagers held in his honor. The year was 1943, the village's name was St. Nazaire, and the airman's name was Alan Magee.

❹ The fried fugu is cash in advance.

The leading theory on how to make zombies probably belongs to Wade Davis, a Harvard-trained Ph.D., who speculates that tetrodotoxin, an incredibly powerful neurotoxin, is the key ingredient in "zombie powder." Neurotoxins are poisons that act on the nervous system and paralyze the victim. You see them a lot in fugu, a fish that has been eaten in Japan for thousands of years. In order to prepare fugu, by the way, a chef has to undertake years of special training before becoming fugu-licensed. The liver of the fish, where the poison is located, has to be very precisely removed with a special knife. One drop of tetrodotoxin is deadly, which is, incidentally, the reason that the emperor of Japan cannot legally eat fugu. Too risky.

❺ Is your love like the countless stars?

Assuming you're far from city lights on a perfectly clear night, you'll be able to see approximately 2,000 stars. You can count them in about twenty minutes.

Five More Facts You Need to Know

6 **Models available in standard and turbo.** A guy in Belgium builds and sells a machine that makes poop. This may sound a little disgusting, but it's actually not; it's art. Called a Cloaca machine, it has been displayed in museums in Europe and New York. It gets fed restaurant leftovers and then, after about 3 hours, it produces the result. This last step is the highlight of the show. A crowd gathers around the

The Cloaca machine

glass-enclosed rear end and breaks into applause at the appropriate moment. The inventor's name is Wim Delvoye and you can buy samples of his machine's output on his website. The machine itself is also for sale. Two hundred thousand dollars for the new "turbo" model.

7 There are:
1,000,000,000,000,000,000,000,000,000,000,000,000,000, 000,000,000,000,000,000,000,000,000,000,000,000,000
atoms in the universe.

10,000,000,000,000,000,000,000,000,000 of them are in you.

8 Meet Thomas Crapper, Plumbing Pioneer. It almost hurts to say this, but Thomas Crapper (1836–1910) did not invent the flush toilet. However, more than any other man, he did the most to popularize it. He was the owner of many patents in the toilet and plumbing area, the first to build a showroom for plumbing fixtures, and his London-based plumbing company, Thomas Crapper and Co., was prominent throughout the latter half of the 19th century.

Not coincidentally, Thomas Crapper is also the patron saint of nominative determinism (where your name steers you in certain career directions). Other famous examples: J. W. Splatt, a prominent British urologist, and Cardinal Sin, a former Archbishop in the Philippines.

9 The Only Permanent Thing Humans Have Ever Done. This dusty bootprint left by Buzz Aldrin on the surface of the moon is makind's most durable construction. Since the moon has no atmosphere, animals, or clumsy tourists, this bootprint should last until the sun explodes (about 5 billion years).

10 Big Art for Big Money. The artist's name is Renee (no last name) and she lives in Toledo Ohio — at the zoo, where she likes to eat about 80 pounds of hay before picking up a brush in her nose which, since Renee's an elephant, is about 4 feet long. Renee is one of the best-known painting elephants, but there are actually many. Check out the Elephant Art Conservatory Project for a broad selection of available elephant art (some of which, you may be glad to know, is done on paper made from elephant dung).

Price range: $300–$10,000

Annie Oakley meets Orville Redenbacher

Mouth Shots

This is an activity that lives on the line between aerodynamics and eating.

Place popcorn on back of fingertips as shown. Line up carefully with mouth.

Smack the back of your wrist with your other hand. The snapback action will kick the kernel into your mouth if you've aimed well, or forehead if you haven't.

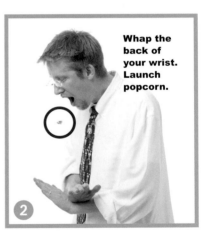

Whap the back of your wrist. Launch popcorn.

Bingo. In mouth.

Winning strategies

Completely Armless Jacket Fights

The next time you're standing around in a group outside, you could make pleasant conversation with the others — attempting to build friendships and community — or you could do what we always do: Start flailing your empty jacket arms at everybody else.

If you choose to start friendly conversations, we have no advice to offer. You're on your own. However, if you choose to start swinging your jacket arms, we have a few valuable pointers.

DO
Twist from
your hips.
Keep your
feet pointed
at your
opponent.

DO
Be aggressive.
Keep your feet
moving forward.

DON'T
Turn your back.
Always face
your opponent.

Paper surgery
Xtreme Makeovers

If you've ever wanted a weird mouth, a huge ear, a massive nose, or just a bizarre jaw, you've come to the right page. Instead of paying big bucks to some fancy plastic surgeon, just cut on the dotted line and paste the picture to the bottom of a paper cup. Take a drink and get someone to shoot a cell phone shot. For the weird ear, nose, and mouth stuff… just hold the book up as shown, no cutting necessary. Send us the photographs. We love this kind of stuff.

Cut along dotted line.

Glue to cup bottom.

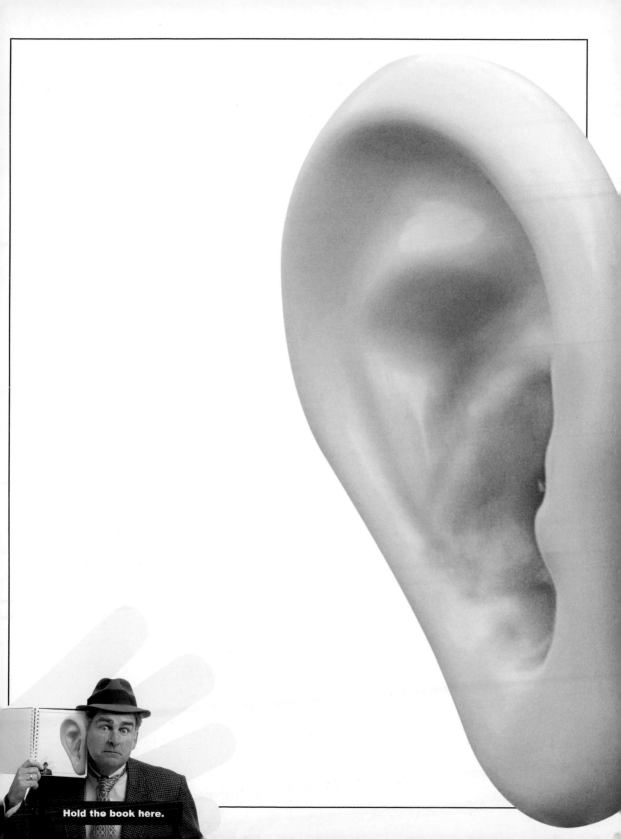

Hold the book here.

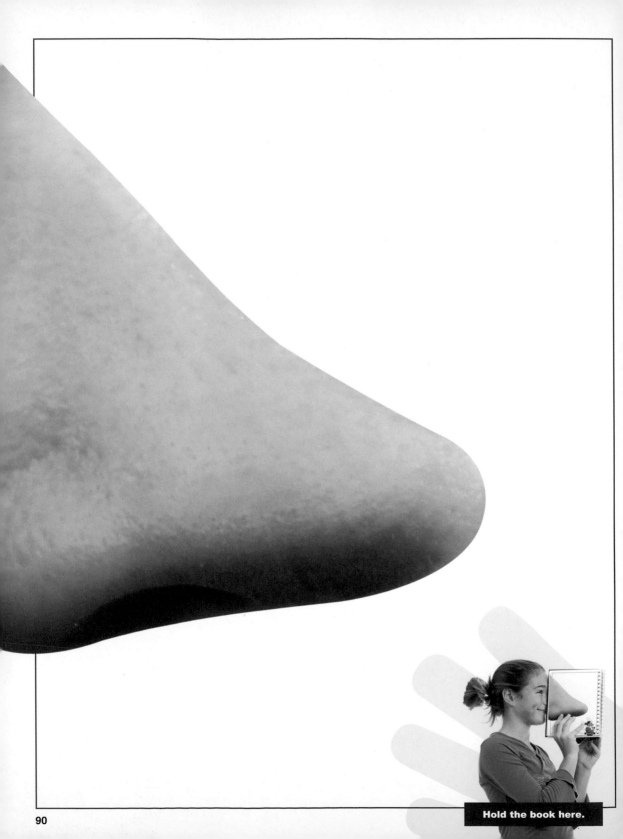

Hold the book here.

Hold the book here.

This Page Is a Human Mouse Trap

Photocopy the facing page. Smear Vaseline or lip balm or something else slimy and disgusting on the black dot. Place in some high traffic area. Wait for results.

DON'T TOUCH THIS DOT!!

WET INK

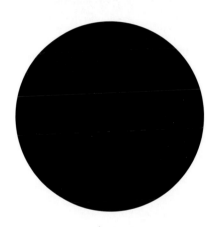

How to Play Table Top Hockey

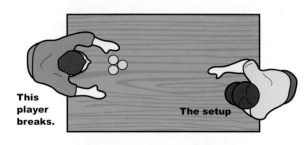

This player breaks.

The setup

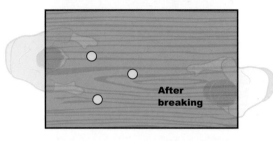

After breaking

When you're ready to move beyond table top football, we have an alternative: table top hockey. You'll need three coins, a table, and an opponent. You shoot the "puck" not by thumping it (like table top football) but sliding it (think shuffleboard). The goal is to stick it into the "net" (your opponent makes one with his hand). The trick is that every shot has to split the gap for you to keep your turn. (See the illustrations, it'll make more sense.) Any misses mean the turn goes over.

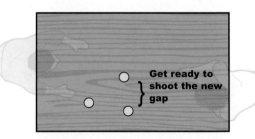

This player shoots again.

Shoot the gap

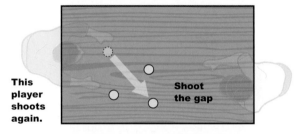

Get ready to shoot the new gap

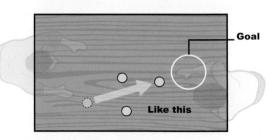

Goal

Like this

How to Find Big Money

Maybe a friend of yours is having a bad day and you're feeling their pain. Would finding a hundred dollar bill cheer them up? Let's find out!

HOW TO GLUE COINS TO THE SIDEWALK

As long as you're up leaving fake bills around, why not glue a few coins to the sidewalk, too? Super Glue is the only way to go. Follow instructions so you don't stick your fingers together (the stuff is REALLY sticky!).

Here's a little note to help you feel better.
Signed,
Thinking of You

Cut this out. Fold on the dotted line. Then put a paper clip over the photo and leave it for a friend to find.

Tricky Stickers

Photocopy this page and tape these down wherever it seems to make good sense. You can tape the "PUSH" sticker on a book cover if you want to be mysteriously arty, or on top of the "PULL" sign on a door if you just want to be annoying. Up to you.

The "Lick" sticker just goes on any ice cream that's in the freezer. Very simple.

P
U
S
H

P
U
L
L

STAY
AWAY!

I'VE
ALREADY
LICKED
THIS.

Always use these stickers as a pair.
On swinging glass doors.

Works on flagpoles, too

How to Shinny Up a Tree

Skinny trees without low branches can be climbed the same way flagpoles can, using the classic shinny technique demonstrated below.

1. Lock on with your legs.

2. Release with your arms and stretch up.

3. Lock on with your arms and bring your feet up. Repeat.

And good morning to YOU!

Frozen Underpants

If you put underpants (not yours) in a freezer overnight, whoever puts them on the next morning will experience a thrill similar to that of an atomic wedgie. Works far better than coffee for providing that early morning "pick-me-up."

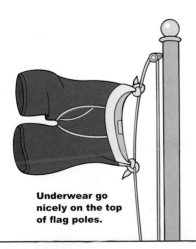

Underwear go nicely on the top of flag poles.

Don't forget to dampen them first. This is important.

99

Without taking off your pants

How to Take Off Your Underpants

This is an activity that lives in the overlap between underpants and athletics. Nobody knows exactly who did the original research, but scientists and many dedicated amateurs have proven that it is possible to remove your underpants without first removing your regular pants. It takes "comfortable" boxers, semi-baggy pants, and a bit of flexibility, but it can be done. We've seen it with our own eyes and offer here the instructions.

Push down to knee.

1

Reach up and grab.

2

Stretch down.

3

Stick foot through.

4

5

Halftime break.

6

Reach down and grab.

7

Pull up. And push down the other leg.

8

Reach up and grab.

9

Pull down...

10

...and out.

11

How to Throw a Boomerang

Because of the fact that boomerangs are really just flat sticks that have been hot-rodded to fly, they are incredibly old technology. The original "Australian flying sticks" were meant to be thrown at flocks of birds with the hope of knocking one down. They were not, by the way, designed to come directly back to the thrower since weapons that come hurtling back at the hunter would be, for obvious reasons, flawed design.

Modern boomerangs, on the other hand, are sporty, not weapony, and are designed to do exactly that. Skilled boomerangers can keep two or three boomerangs going at once, juggling them over a 40-yard field.

THE TECHNIQUE:
Throw more like a baseball than a frisbee.
Snap your wrist to give it a lot of spin.

HOW TO RELEASE YOUR BOOMERANG: THE ANGLE IS KEY

Release the boomerang at this angle.

🚫 Don't release it at a vertical angle.

Grip it like this.

🚫 And don't release at a flat angle.

WHERE TO GET YOUR BOOMERANG

Go online. There are tons of websites. The triblades are easier to throw and more reliable. They just don't look like a classic boomerang. And if you're a lefty, you'll have to buy special.

The Big Sneeze

Put a spoon in your mouth and cover your nose with the napkin they have at restaurants. Fake a sneeze and twang up the spoon.

achoo!

How to Cure the Hiccups

More than a hundred hiccup cures are described in the literature and online. They vary from holding your breath to swallowing a teaspoonful of sugar to sticking your fingers in your ears. Others involve tickling the roof of your mouth or taking antacids. Despite their huge variety, all of them do share one thing in common, though; they are offered by people who are truly trying to help.

And that's where our cures differ.

Because we just made ours up out of thin air. Completely untested. Who knows if they'll work? That's not really why we're here. We're here to see if you can get some of your friends to do these things when they get the hiccups. If you do, take a picture and email it to us. We'd love to see it.

1. Stand up on one foot and puff out your cheeks alternately, left, right, left, right… until the hiccups stop.

2. Take a huge breath, throw your head way back and holler "ahhhhhhh… gugggagugga… ahhhhhhh…" Continue as long as necessary until the problem ceases.

3. Crouch low and leap into the air repeatedly and rapidly, every time exhaling "huhhh" when you hit the ground.

4. Shake your head violently left to right while allowing your cheeks to fully relax so they are free to make a wobble wobble kind of noise.

5. Close your eyes and count to 1,000, clapping both your cupped hands smartly over your ears with each count.

998… 999… 1,000.

The History of Flip-Flop Mail

The first volume of this encyclopedia challenged our readers to mail us their retired, unpackaged flip-flops upon which were written "first-time sentences": sentences that "had never before been used or written in the history of the English language." The response has been enormously gratifying and in the intervening months we have received many deeply moving submissions. The sentences have made for a different kind of reading experience and the daily flow of old flip-flops has in many ways enriched our relationship with the U.S.P.S.

We continue to welcome flip-flop mail. Please send us yours. But, we also offer here an alternative (see next page).

Send Us a Message in a Bottle

Like most people, we love flip-flop mail and have been receiving lots of it from readers of the first volume of this encyclopedia. But for this volume, we'd like to start a new tradition: messages in a bottle.

If you can answer the following three questions accurately and completely, using no words that contain either a "P" or an "O" and that fit onto a postcard, we will send you a certificate that says something nice about you. Suitable for framing.

1 What do a lot of dogs do when they see a water hydrant?

2 What color is this?

3 What are those guys called who wear patches over their eyes and say "Aaaaaaargh" and sail around in ships with flags like these?

How to Clap Launch a Plastic Top

Little tricks like this one are fantastic for creating the illusion of mysterious powers or mad skills. They take about 3 minutes to learn, but since no one else can do them, you look like a Houdini.

Do this first. Cup your hands together and clap them so they make that hollow sound. (It's different from regular clapping.) Remember that sound. You're going to need it in a minute.

1. Make a loose fist. (Call it a hollow fist.)

2. Put a plastic bottle top on top of it and "screw" it in lightly so it seals. (Lightly, not tightly)

3. Cup your other hand and…

4. Strike the bottom of your hollow fist so that you get that hollow sound we talked about a minute ago. The top will go rocketing off and hit the ceiling, like a cork out of champagne.

FAQ. I tried it and nothing happened. Or the cap just kind of fell off.

That's because you're not cupping your bottom hand like we told you at the beginning. Go back and do the practice step to remind yourself what we're talking about.

P.S. Don't give this away.

The key thing, and the reason no one else will be able to do it unless you give it away and show them, is to clap your bottom hand against your fist so that it makes a hollow, resonant sound.

A contest you can win

Do Your Feet Stink?

We have a contest here you should enter. If you're the kind of person who reads this kind of book, we think you have a real shot at this one. Here are the rules.

1 Cut this out and put it in your shoe for awhile. Quite awhile.

2 Mail it to us straight. No envelopes. We will carefully judge each of the entries and if your card makes the grade, we will send you our "I Have Really Stinky Feet" certificate, suitable for framing.

By the way, if you never hear from us… sorry… you've lost another contest.

STAMP

KLUTZ®

**450 Lambert
Palo Alto, CA
94306**

OFFICIAL
STINKY FOOT
CONTEST
CONTEST

The classic

Putting on a Kick Me Sticker

1 **Inspire trust. Offer chair.**

2 **Place sticker.**

BIO-
HAZARD
LEVEL 4
HOW DO YOU
LIKE MY
WALKING
?
1-800-DONTCARE
FREE
PIGGY-
BACKS!
HOP
ON!
EXPLOSIVES
STAY
BACK!
MAKES
WIDE
TURNS
BLASTING
ZONE

How to Fake a Sword Fight

EN GARDE

It's important to move your feet and clash swords high and low. Decide how many times in advance. Do a lot of grunting.

SWEEP AND LEAP

The sweeper needs to "telegraph" his move with a huge wind-up. As soon as the leaper gets into the air, the sweeper has to whip through the gap or he'll land on the sword.

The world of "stage combat" is a big one. In Hollywood, professional fight coordinators are busy every day helping actors take a swing at each other. And miss.

It's an art and a science, but what follow are a few of the very basics for good-looking, fake sword fighting. Makes a terrific home video when you get it down.

You'll need cardboard tubes.

THRUST AND PARRY

The guy on defense should start this move by leaning back. On offense, you need to "telegraph" your move with a big wind-up.

TOUCHÉ

Like a band that knows when to end the song together, you and your partner need to decide in advance when to close it out. Practice makes perfect. Don't forget the sound effects.

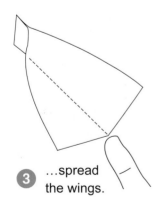

How to Make a Sticky Note Paper Airplane

1 Start with a 3 x 3 sticky note with the adhesive facing up. Fold it in half on the dotted line.

2 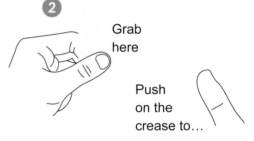 Grab here

Push on the crease to…

3 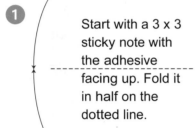 …spread the wings.

4 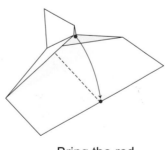 Bring the red dots together.

5 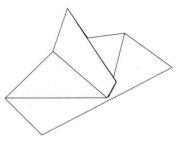 End up like this.

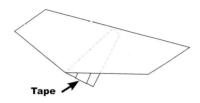

Tape

6 Turn over, and add 2 or 3 pieces of tape as shown just on the nose. It's for weight. Make everything neat, flat, and precise.

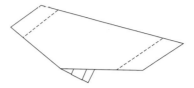

7 Bend on dotted lines.

Forward view

Use a gentle, straight ahead toss. Add another piece of nose tape and tweak up the wings if it just crashes and burns. It should be good for 10-foot flights.

Tweak the wings up on the area tinted green.

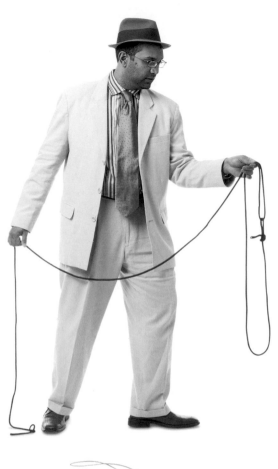

How to Make a Lasso

Millions of kids these days, who are thinking and concerned about their futures, are torn between two of the most attractive career options available in our fast-moving 21st century world. Pirate or cowboy? What's it going to be?

Naturally, we can't make these hard choices for you, but we can give you a chance to test-drive the options. Here are the steps for learning how to lasso. Turn to page 112 for learning how to wield a saber.

①

②

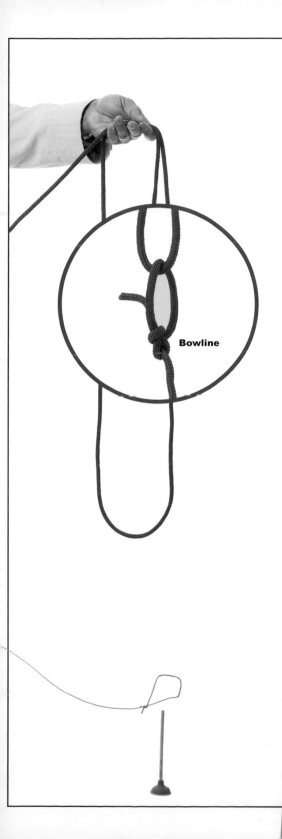

Bowline

HOW TO TIE THE BOWLINE

Follow the red end. It comes through the hole…

…around the "tree"…

The tree

…and back through the hole.

You've now made the little loop. It's tinted pink in the photograph.

This is what it looks like upside down as in the photograph.

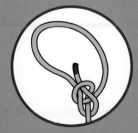

How to Slip on a Banana Peel

We have enormous respect for the genius behind this activity. Our entire life we've been watching people slip on banana peels and fall down painfully. But all we've done is slapped a knee heartily and laughed, never stopping to think: What are the implications here… where can we take this?

1 Eat a banana.

2 Split the peel into four and stick them under your chair legs.

3 Go sliding around the floor. Or get your friend to push you.

It works incredibly well.

After you're done, some observant mothers might notice a slight trail of banana slime which dries and becomes a little sticky. If it helps, you can tell her the people at Klutz just ignore it.

◁ **Note banana peels.**

Two Mentos®
hanging on
a thread. The
key ingredient.

How to Booby Trap a Drink

1 Make a hole in a couple of Mentos® and thread them onto some dental floss.

2 Open a bottle of diet soda and hang the Mentos just inside the cap.

3 Screw the cap back on and trim off the hanging piece of dental floss.

4 Give to friend. And start backing away.

X-ray view.
Mentos hanging
just inside cap.

How to Be a Stickpocket

Stickpockets are like pickpockets only different: they put things **into** people's pockets… things like pickles and leftovers and odd pieces of underwear. Or, just use it to get rid of any trash when you can't find a garbage can.

Identify victim.

Case the situation.

Distract.

Deposit pickle. *

*Ice cube, banana peel, old underwear, etc.

How to Hypnotize a Chicken

This item is for everyone who believes that life on the farm just isn't interesting enough. It turns out that chickens are remarkably hypnotizable. Many systems seem to work; here are two.

You will need: a chicken.

1 Put the chicken on the ground so its "chin" is laying on the ground and it is staring straight ahead. (Same pose you see in the cop shows when the suspect is laying on the ground in handcuffs.)

2 Draw a straight line in the dirt right in front of its nose (OK, beak).

3 Done. You can let go. Clap your hands to break the spell.

Plan B.

1 Lay the chicken on the ground on its back so it is staring at the sky.

2 Draw circles in the air with your finger right in front of its eyes.

3 Done. You can let go. Clap your hands to break the spell.

Why Does This Man Have Candy on His Nose?

We've all seen dogs who can balance a dog biscuit on their nose and then, at a command, toss it up and snatch it in mid-air. An impressive dog trick. This is a very similar item except it's your friend and a piece of candy.

1 Get a friend to balance a piece of candy on their nose.

2 Make everyone else watch and then holler, "Eat!"

3 Now your friend is supposed to flip it up and snarf it down. No hands. Whether it works or not is not important since it's pretty funny regardless.

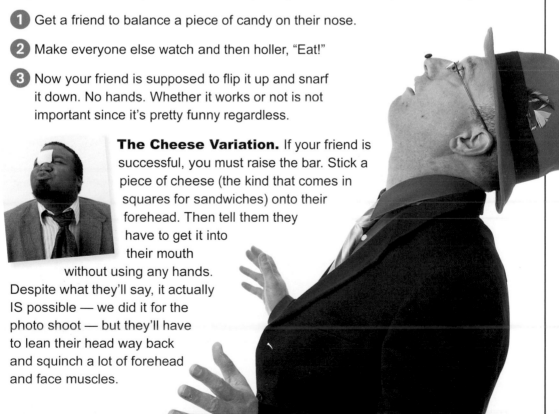

The Cheese Variation. If your friend is successful, you must raise the bar. Stick a piece of cheese (the kind that comes in squares for sandwiches) onto their forehead. Then tell them they have to get it into their mouth without using any hands. Despite what they'll say, it actually IS possible — we did it for the photo shoot — but they'll have to lean their head way back and squinch a lot of forehead and face muscles.

The Elephant of Surprise

The dictionary meaning of the word "startle" is "to jump in surprise or alarm." But those are just words. To get a deeper, gut-level understanding of the word, try putting a cardboard tube by someone's ear and saying, "Boo!"

And other messes

How to Make Bird Poop

Spill a good-looking plop of Elmer's on a piece of waxed paper. The shape matters so look at the photo. Add a few bits of dirt, unmixed. Again, this is slow-dry. Figure a few days in a warm room.

In a coffee cup mix Elmer's white glue with a few drops of brown acrylic paint. Then dump onto a sheet of wax paper and let dry (which can take days if your room is cold). Add a coffee stirrer or spoon if you're a stickler for realism.

How to Juggle Clubs

THE ONE CLUB FLIP:
RIGHT TO LEFT
You have to learn this deeply. One flip from hand to hand.

The flight plan.

One single perfect spin.

A perfect toss makes the catch automatic.

THE ONE CLUB FLIP:
LEFT TO RIGHT

You have to learn this deeply, too. The club should hit your hand perfectly.

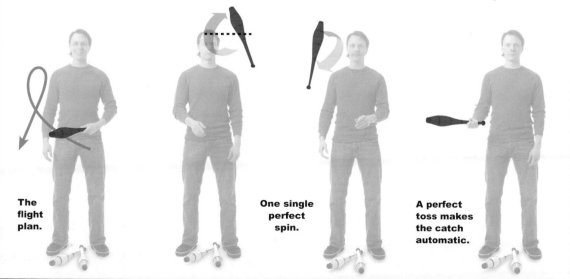

The flight plan.

One single perfect spin.

A perfect toss makes the catch automatic.

HOW TO LEARN TO JUGGLE

The big secret? Bean bags or socks stuffed with rice. Tennis balls are incredibly frustrating because they bounce and roll away when they're dropped and trust us, you'll be dropping a lot.

The motion is exactly the same as clubs... up from one hand, then after it tops out on its little arc, toss another bag up and catch the first. The key is to make the tosses extremely catchable. You should have to reach for nothing.

THE EXCHANGE:
Swapping a flying club for a held club.

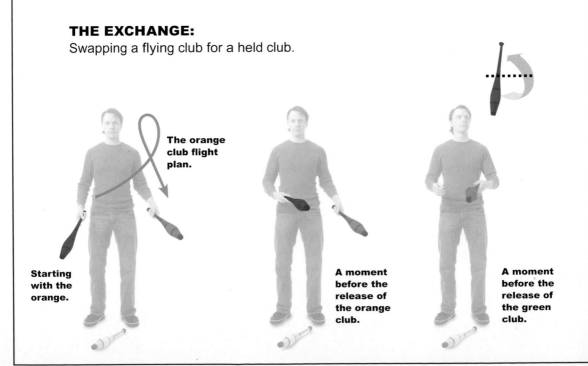

The orange club flight plan.

Starting with the orange.

A moment before the release of the orange club.

A moment before the release of the green club.

Every toss goes up; no toss goes straight between the hands. Up, up, and up. Some people learn in an hour or two; others take days. It's about as hard as learning how to ride a two-wheeler the first time.

Our experience, by the way, makes us think that people younger than 9 or 10 will be very challenged. It's a better big kid activity.

The exchange. Orange club headed in. Green club headed out.

Green club comes in...

...and lands.

THE JUG:
Putting two exchanges back-to-back

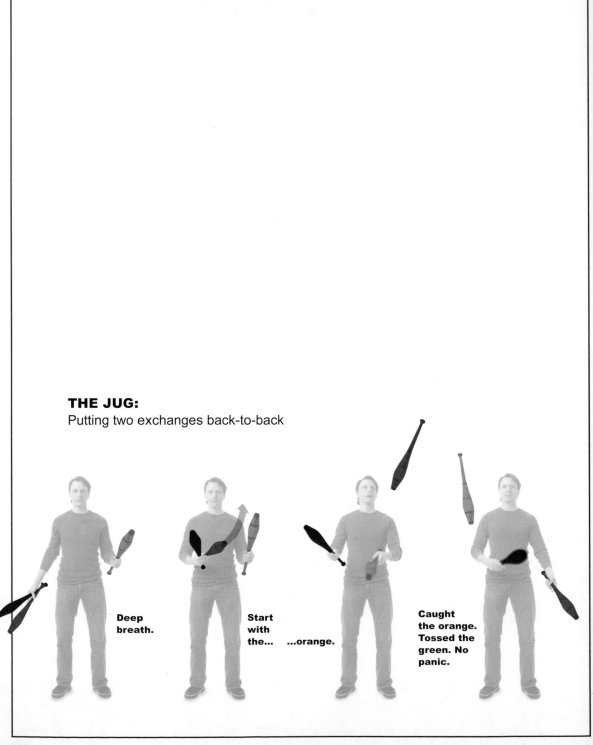

Deep
breath.

Start
with
the...   ...orange.

Caught
the orange.
Tossed the
green. No
panic.

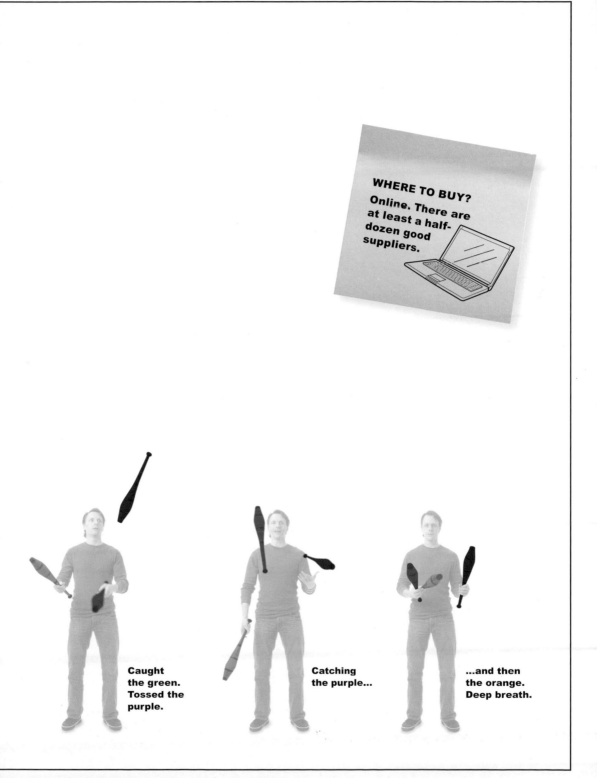

WHERE TO BUY?
Online. There are at least a half-dozen good suppliers.

Caught the green. Tossed the purple.

Catching the purple...

...and then the orange. Deep breath.

Night Writing

A lot of point-and-shoot cameras have a button that lets you leave the shutter open for as long as 30 seconds. If you have a flashlight and a camera with a feature like that, you have the fixings for light writing. It's like sky writing, only at night. And no airplane needed.

1. Set the camera up pointing into the pitch dark somewhere. The darker, the better.

2. Punch the button that leaves the shutter open for 30 seconds or so.

3. Jump in front of the camera, turn on your flashlight, and write something in mid-air. If you finish before the camera clicks, just freeze until it does.

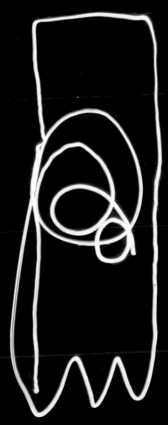

Ten Things You're Not Supposed to Know

1 In old buildings, you can "hack" the elevator by pushing your floor simultaneously with the "close" button. You'll go straight to your floor.

2 Cold weather doesn't make you more liable to get a cold. Drinking more fluids, or taking extra vitamin C, doesn't help, either.

3 Cats will get disoriented if you put packing tape on their backs.

4 Dollar bills are actually worthless. They're like notes to Santa. They're only good if your parents (and the rest of the world) plays along with the joke.

5 The water in airplane bathrooms is dangerous to drink.

6 The origin of the Barbie doll was a German men's gag gift.

7 Human brains begin to deteriorate after the age of 18.

8 If you put a small piece of paper, that's been laminated with plastic, on a string around your neck, and carry a clipboard, you'll be "authorized personnel." Handy for going backstage and places like that.

9 40% of fresh human poop is alive.

10 Most crosswalk turn-the-light buttons are worthless. They don't work. They weren't even meant to.

Going beyond Aaaaaarrr

How to Talk Like a Pirate

Connect the dots. Answers on page 197.

❶ Avast
 or Belay

❷ Ahoy

❸ Scuttle

❹ Bucko

❺ Abaft

❻ Booty

❼ Smart

❽ Aloft

❾ Lubber

❿ Beauty

⓫ Weigh anchor
 or cast off

⓬ Aye

⓭ Matey

⓮ Me

Ⓐ Behind

Ⓑ Yes

Ⓒ Someone who
 lives on land

Ⓓ Loot

Ⓔ Cut that out!

Ⓕ Howdy

Ⓖ My

Ⓗ Guy you've
 just met

Ⓘ Call off

Ⓙ Good Pal

Ⓚ Girl

Ⓛ Quickly

Ⓜ Up above

Ⓝ Leave

OFFICIAL
TALK LIKE
A PIRATE
DAY

SEPT.
19

How to Play with Your Food

Most of this material you probably already know, but we include it here since it's easy to forget and it never hurts to review the basics.

KNOCK OUT YOUR FRONT TOOTH

There are a couple of ways to get this look. If you're really short you can stand in front of a door until someone opens it and the doorknob gets you. Or, if you're too tall for that, you can stick a raisin over your teeth. Like we did here.

LAGGING JOLLY RANCHERS

Stand back from a wall. Toss your Jolly Rancher as close to it as you can. Your opponent does the same. Closest to the wall takes both.

MASHED POTATO SCULPTURE

EGG SHELL EYES

Ping-pong halves work pretty well, too.

HOW TO DEFUSE A SHAKEN SODA CAN

If you thump the top with a finger a few times, and wait about 20 seconds, you can open a shaken can safely.

POTATO CHIP DUCK LIPS

Orange Peel Dentures

If you're tired of paying big bucks to get your teeth whitened, or if you're just trying to get your teeth to make more of a statement about who you are, this could be your item.

(P.S. Our photographer, a seasoned professional, had to be led from the studio until he could recover himself enough to take this picture. It's that funny.)

Cut and peel one section of orange. Cut teeth. Wear with pride.

Cut in half.

In half again.

Peel.

Trim off the points.

Like so.

Cut teeth.

Done.

Pretty tasty

How to Eat Scabs

Admit it. You're reading this with fear. You're worried this isn't a trick. You're worried where this might go…

A 4th-grade friend of ours, Dickie Rajoppi, claims to have invented this one, but in fairness there may have been others. Great discoveries are often made simultaneously and independently. The calculus, for example, appears to have been invented simultaneously by Isaac Newton in England and Gottfried Leibniz in Germany.

It's the same with eating scabs. Dickie may have been doing his work at the same time as others. In any event, it was an idea whose time had come. Here are the steps.

1 Take a piece of fruit leather and work a small piece of it onto your knee or elbow until it looks like an incredibly realistic scab.

2 Then, when others are watching, start to pick at it and finally, peel the whole thing off and eat it, smacking your lips at the end. Yummy!

The Fisherman's Handshake

We find this to be a fresh alternative to the conventional style, which we are frankly weary of. Grab the guy by the thumb and reel him in.

See explanatory pictures below.

Cell phone puppetry

How to Throw Your Voice for Miles

Maybe you've seen ventriloquists on TV who can make their dummies tell dumb jokes and do impressions of famous people and otherwise be the life of the party. And maybe you've secretly wished you could be a dummy too someday?

Well, you can! And here's how! Two systems: One, you can train for years so that you can talk without moving your lips. Or, two, you can get a cell phone like we did and cheat!

1 Get a sock and put two eyes on it.

2 Get a cellphone that has a speaker function. Ours doesn't, but someone in our office had one. Find your own and get someone to call you on it.

3 Then, put it inside the sock and you're good to go. Bring in the audience. It helps to fake move your mouth a little bit when your sock dummy is talking. Just a little. Otherwise they might get suspicious.

The secret

YOUR SOCK: I just moved into a new shoe. He stinks!

YOU: That's too bad. What are you going to do about it?

YOUR SOCK: I'm switching places with my twin brother.

YOU: I didn't know you had a twin brother.

YOUR SOCK: I just found him in the dryer. We were separated at spin and rinse.

YOU: Family is so important. Why don't you sing the people a song about that? While I have a drink here…

YOUR SOCK: [sings] We Are Family

How to Walk a Slackline

Tightrope walking is an ancient activity that goes back to our days in the trees when the ropes were branches. These days, performing tightrope walkers use wires. But slackline walking is done on nylon webbing — the material used in car seat belts only thinner. You can get it at outdoor stores but it's best to go online and buy a slackline which comes with the hardware you need to tighten it up enough. Unfortunately, it's almost impossible to get the line tight enough without the special hardware no matter how hard you pull. The line has to be strung as tight as a bowstring, otherwise it'll stretch straight to the ground when you step on it.

Protect the tree by using cardboard.

YOUR FIRST STEP
Step on the line…

…and step off.
Repeat, repeat, repeat.

THE SHIMMY SHIMMY LEG

The shimmy shimmy leg happens to everybody. Your leg will start to wobble wildly side to side. To stop it…

…put a hand on the tree and push down with your foot. You'll bounce up and down a little bit, but that's easier to control than the side-to-side shimmy.

3

NEXT STEP
Get a friend. Just lean on his shoulder. Don't grab it.

4

You'll take a step and fall off. Repeat, repeat, repeat.

Walking on a slackline hung low to the ground is a much more recent phenomenon. Only in the last 30 years has it really hit the radar as a campground, front yard (or even dorm room) activity. In its current form, it probably started amongst the rock-climbers where it still enjoys enormous popularity. It's one of those skills that looks completely impossible and for the first hour or two feels like it, too. But, miraculously, it turns out to be not too bad — about like an average skateboard trick. On the other hand, it's definitely not easy, and there is no magic pill except the one called Practice. Take every day.

YOUR SECOND STEP
After a while, your friend will get tired of helping you. Your first solo step will have to follow. It will probably take hours of falling.

REST MODE
Balancing on one foot is much more stable.

SAFETY: The rope is traditionally only a foot or two off the ground at its lowest, so you won't need drumrolls or a safety net. But still, awkward dangerous falls are quite possible even at that height and you should definitely start with something to hang onto. The slackline equivalent of training wheels.

TIP

Don't look at your feet or the other tree. Keep your eyes on the line a few feet in front of you.

OUR MOST IMPORTANT TIP
Bend your knees to stabilize
yourself. This really, really works.

How to Kick a Footbag

Footbag is just like juggling with one catch: no hands. The entire sport is built around three basic kicks: inside, outside, and back. (It's like tennis. Forehand, backhand, and overhead.)

What follow are the basic instructions. But before you start you should learn the traditional beginning footbagger's motto since you'll be saying it a lot. It goes: "Wow. This sure seems completely impossible."

THE INSIDE KICK

DO bend your ankle

DON'T leave it like this

It's not, actually. But at first it'll definitely seem that way.
Practice in small bites and get together with a friend
so you can start popping it back and forth, foot to foot.
You'd be amazed what you'll be doing after a few days.

THE OUTSIDE KICK

Get into position.

Lean away from the
footbag and lift (don't
kick or swat) your foot.

Do it right, and
the footbag pops
straight up.

THE BACK KICK

Get into position.
The footbag is headed
for a point behind you.
Not beside you.

Lean away from
the footbag and
lift (don't kick or
swat) your foot.

Contact the footbag
waist high.

How to Play "Oh Susanna" on the Harmonica

It's traditional to make *Oh Susanna* your first harmonica tune. Nobody knows why, everybody just does it.

4 ④ 5   6   ⑥ 6 5 4   ④   5   ④ 4 ④

Well I come from Alabama with my banjo on my knee

4 ④ 5 6   ⑥ 6 5 4 ④   5   4 ④   4

And I'm going to Louisiana oh my true love for to see.

⑤   ⑥   ⑥   6   5 4 ④

Oh Susanna! Oh don't you cry for me.

4 ④   5   6   ⑥ 6 5 4 ④   5   4 ④   4

For I'm bound for Louisiana oh my true love for to see.

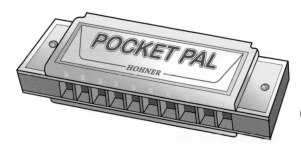

4 means blow on the 4 hole.

④ means suck or draw on the 4 hole.

How to 360 a Scooter

The world of freestyle scooter is enormous but the entry level trick is the 360° spin. It's the one you'll have to learn just to get into the game. There's no magic pill to scooter tricks except the one called practice: Take one every day.

To stick a 360°, you'll need to be rolling steadily. Then bend your knees and bounce while you pull the scooter up with you. Then with your feet, kick it around and land it perfectly. (Or at least try… figure on days of practice.)

How to Make an Altoid® Robot

It always feels particularly bad to get rid of an old Altoid tin, even in the recycling bin. No doubt many people use them to safekeep coins and so forth, but we've always been seeing faces and legs on ours. Since we've been buying them for years, our teeth are now rotting but our desk is home to a small battalion of fighting Altoid robots. The instructions are as follows: Use glue and stick things onto them.

Bead

Wire

Brads

Eraser

Staples

You don't really need instructions, do you?

How to Amputate Your Leg

And comb kazoo

How to Play the Spoons

Everybody should know how to play at least one instrument and the spoons, we believe, are your entry-level place in the band. They qualify as the last resort for people who have musically given up on themselves. They make a tambourine look tough.

Hold them as shown and tap them in time between the heel of your hand and your knee. You can just go click-click-click (like tapping your foot) or you can get into fancy rhythms if you're that kind of person.

(You'd be amazed how good they can sound. Go online to check it out.)

How to Make and Use a Tennis Ball Bola

Nothing is more exciting than a good old fashioned ancient weapon. Like most people, our blood starts to race whenever we think of atlatls, nunchakus, maces, flails, slings, catapults, and all that sort of thing. They were all high technology back in the days when the guy who invented the big stick was still a famous scientist.

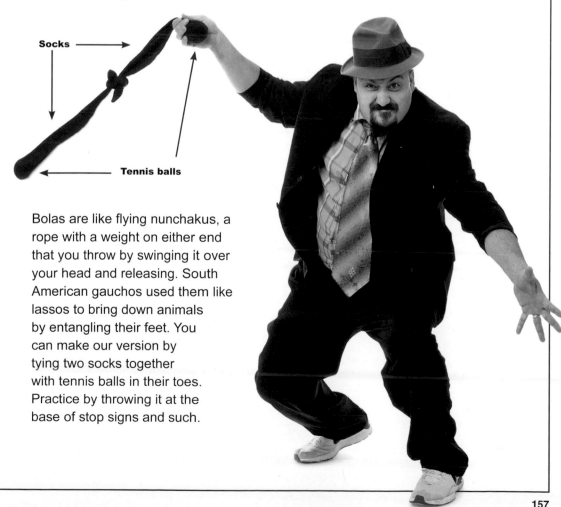

Socks →

Tennis balls ←

Bolas are like flying nunchakus, a rope with a weight on either end that you throw by swinging it over your head and releasing. South American gauchos used them like lassos to bring down animals by entangling their feet. You can make our version by tying two socks together with tennis balls in their toes. Practice by throwing it at the base of stop signs and such.

How to Be a Plunger Performer

Back in the day, a lot of stage performers used canes to twirl, balance, and flip around. That's fine if you have a cane, but here at Klutz we've learned to make do.

THE CHIN BALANCE
Keep your eyes on the top and bend your knees. It's actually not that tough. It only takes a few minutes of practice.

THE FINGER BALANCE

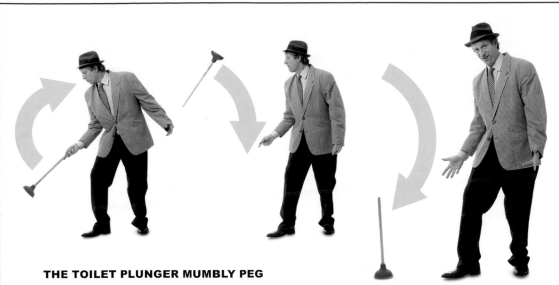

THE TOILET PLUNGER MUMBLY PEG

A single flip is what we illustrate here. But multiple flips are quite possible if you aspire to toilet plunger greatness. Note that success is measured only when the plunger really sticks to the floor.

THE TOILET PLUNGER GARGLE

How to Catch Popcorn on Your Tongue

We used to think that catching food in your mouth was just one of those skills — like being able to curl your tongue — that you either had or didn't. It took Jeff Raz, who teaches clowning in San Francisco, to demonstrate how wrong we were. You can actually achieve greatness at catching food in your mouth if you simply follow Jeff's food-catching rules:

1. Stick your tongue out and catch on your tongue. Not in your mouth.

2. Lock onto your target as it hits the peak of its arc. Don't try to follow it with your eyes all the way in. (Doesn't work and actually creates more problems.)

*Are you ready
for mime time?*

How to
Lean on
Things That
Aren't There

THE SECRET?
A lot of weight
is on this foot.

How to play

Face Horse

You'll need three people for this one. Two players and a referee. It's like basketball horse, only different. Instead of shooting weird baskets, you make weird faces.

We'll make you the first player. Make a face. The other player has to match. Failure to match exactly means that player gets an "H" and you keep your turn. Otherwise, no score and the turn goes over. First person to get "HORSE" by losing five turns is the loser. There will be arguments of course but that's why the referee.

EXAMPLE

Player A challenges

Player B matches

"I Gotta Be Me!"

When you wear an iPod®, where do you put the earbud things? In your ears?

Are you proud of that? Are you tired of looking like a sheep? Are you ready to wear your earbuds in a new way that will say to the world, "I am me!"

1 Stick the earbuds up your nose, as shown.

2 Turn the music up loud.

3 Now, when you sing along, the music will come out of your mouth, nosehole karaoke.*

*OK. Actually, this only works if you cheat. But hey. Push the pause button every time you open your mouth, and then push it again every time you close it. Don't tell people you are doing this, by the way, it's a "secret."

The Egg and Shirt Throw

Most people think it's quite difficult to throw an egg really really hard without breaking it. But that's because most people aren't as well-informed about the ballistics of flying eggs and controlled deceleration as you are. Or will be, as soon as you read what follows.

1 Get a long-sleeved shirt and tie the sleeves and neck as shown.

2 Find someone who will hold it in a doorway as shown. Tell them to hang on tight and hide behind the wall. It's for their own good.

3 Get an egg, step away from the target a few feet and heave it with great velocity at the shirt. Not the wall.

We don't want to give away the end, so we won't tell you what happens next. You'll just have to try it. It's the scientific method.

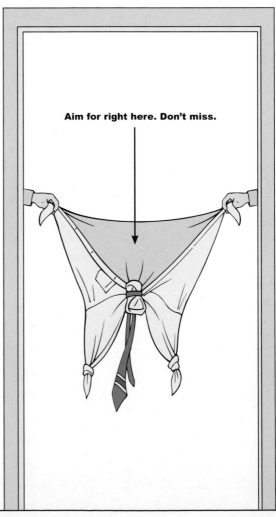

Aim for right here. Don't miss.

Who needs a Frisbee®?

How to Throw Playing Cards

Magicians call it "scaling," the art of zinging a playing card for speed and serious distance. It used to be a basic for vaudeville magicians who wanted to distribute their business cards throughout a huge theatre — including the balcony.

A number of grips and techniques exist in the literature (we're not making this up), but we have found the greatest success with a grip named after magician Ricky Jay, who has written a modern treatise on the subject.

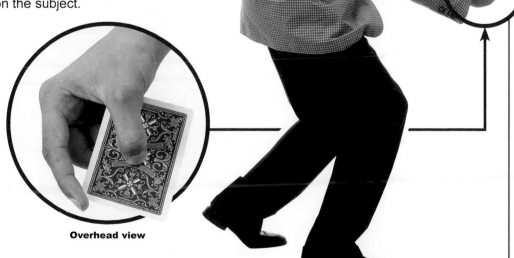

Overhead view

Well, almost

How to Make a Paper Airplane That Flies Forever

This is a paper airplane that lives at the intersection of magic and paper flight. Fold it out of phone directory paper since regular paper is too heavy. As you can see it is shaped like a rectangle with turned-up ends and bent "lips." It falls more than flies and as it falls, it rotates like a log in the water (or a well-behaved leaf). The magic comes when you walk behind it, holding an inclined piece of cardboard. Once you get the knack, you can support it on the updraft as you walk along — a perma-flight paper airplane.

1 Cut a strip of phone book paper exactly like this. Don't use regular paper. Too heavy. Fold at right angles on the dotted lines.

1"

1/2"   1/2"

◄──────────── 4½" ────────────►

Right angle   Right angle

2 If you look at it in profile, it looks like this.
Make the right angles perfect.

3 If you look at it top down, it looks like this.

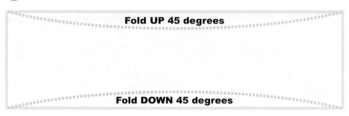

Fold UP 45 degrees

Fold DOWN 45 degrees

Fold along the dotted lines. You'll be folding the lips.
Fold one of them toward you and one of them away.
Use a 45-degree angle. Be precise.

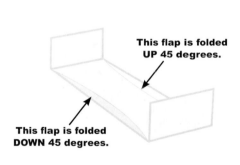

This flap is folded
UP 45 degrees.

This flap is folded
DOWN 45 degrees.

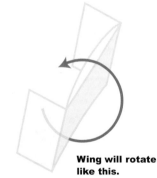

Wing will rotate
like this.

FLIGHT INSTRUCTIONS

Hold the plane above your head and drop it. Give it a little spin as you do this. It should rotate as it falls. Let it get going.

This next step is the toughest. Using a piece of inclined cardboard, walk behind the wing just fast enough so that the updraft supports it. Figure on 10 minutes of practice (it's about like trying to balance a spinning ball on one finger). If you really get stuck, go online. Search "walkalong gliders."

How to Make Pickled Elf Bottoms

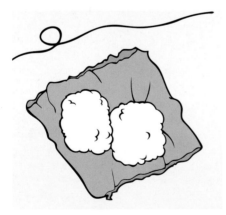

1 Cut the pantyhose into squares, maybe 3 inches on each edge. Lay two cotton balls inside.

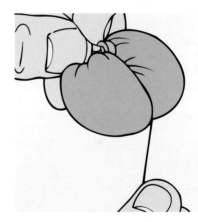

2 Gather into a little sack, and use thread (no needle, no need) to close it up…

In the first volume of this encyclopedia, we included a recipe for shrinking heads. Many of our readers have written in to ask: Now that I've shrunk the head, what do I do with the leftovers?

Good question. And it shows you're concerned about waste. We suggest you pickle the bottoms and present them as a holiday or mother's day gift.

You will need one old pair of pantyhose and some cotton balls.

See page 403 in Volume 1 for instructions on how to shrink heads.

3 …and lightly cinch in half.

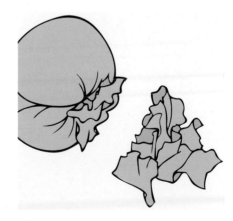

4 Trim off the gathers. Done.

You are getting sleepy

How to Hypnotize a Hot Dog

This is an activity that's a mix of optical illusion, hypnosis, and playing with your food. You are going to need a hot dog and a volunteer who has (at least) one finger.

Make your volunteer put two fingers out on a table, one from each hand. Except one of the fingers isn't a finger; it's a hot dog. Your job is to convince your volunteer otherwise.

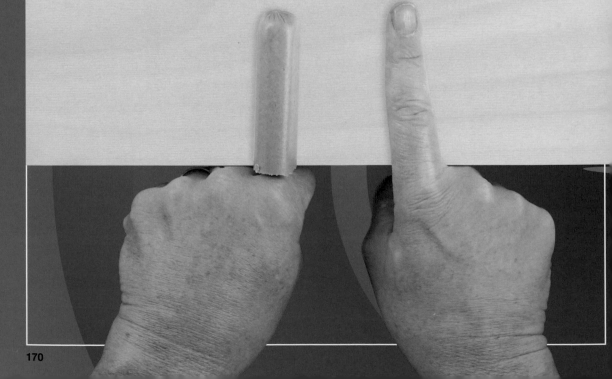

Using a soothing sleepy voice, tell your volunteer that this hot dog he's looking at is actually his finger ("It just *looks* like a hot dog…"). As you're saying that, begin stroking the hot dog at the same time as you're stroking his real finger… ("Can you feel that?"). Do this for a while and then blow on the two of them at the same time ("Can you feel the wind?"). Repeat this a few times and then pick up a big spoon and whap the hot dog. (Note we said "hot dog," not "his finger.")

It's amazing. *Everybody* screams in pain. If you've done a good hypnosis job, that hot dog *is* his finger and he will feel it big time.

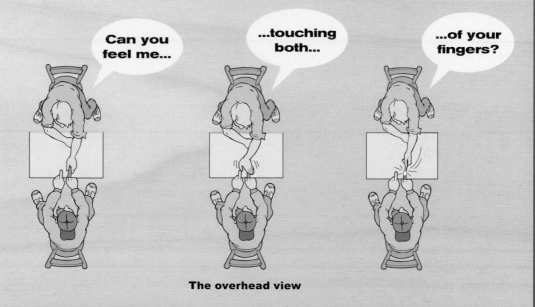

The overhead view

The prize. Grab it first and be the winner.

All the links in the chains except the first keep their eyes closed and hands held.

Pass the Squeeze, Please

The first link. Eyes open.

The first link. Eyes open.

The referee uncovers a coin in her hand. Heads? The squeeze goes. Tails? No squeeze.

Whenever you're in a group bigger than 10 and smaller than 1,000, we have a game you should know. It is our absolute favorite large-group game of all time. It works indoors or out — anywhere, any age. The little kids can mix right in with the old folks. All are equal; it doesn't matter.

1 Create two lines of players, exactly the same number facing each other.

2 Tell everybody in one line to hold the hand of the person next to them.

3 Put a prize like a stuffed toy at the end of the lines.

4 The person at the head of each line is called "the first link." You're the referee. Sit down between them and tell them to keep their eyes hard on you. Everybody else in both lines, tell them to shut their eyes tightly!

5 In your hand you have a coin hidden. When you uncover it, both of the first links will see it. If it is heads, they will squeeze the hand of the second link, who will squeeze the hand of the third link, who will squeeze the hand of the fourth link… etc., etc., all the way to the last link who will snatch the prize as soon as they feel their hand squeezed. The whole thing is like an electricity race and it happens very fast.

6 False starts. When you open your hand and the coin is tails, the first links should NOT squeeze. If one of them does, the squeeze will shoot down the line and a false grab will be made. When that happens, that is a false start and the bad people in that line are penalized one point.

7 When you get a winner, make the first and last links swap places with people in the middle of the line so that everyone gets a turn at the hot spots. We usually play to 5 points or so and it takes 10 to 15 minutes.

Cheating. This happens to us all the time. People in the middle of the chain, who are supposed to keep their eyes closed, will try to peek.

You must be ruthless about this. No peeking! And no fair saying anything! The game is played in complete silence until a winning snatch is made.

The only three things you need to know

How to Be a Magician

The entire world of magic is built on three pillars: One, misdirection. Two, expectation. And three, pixie dust.

About 40 years ago an Israeli/British performer by the name of Uri Geller made a name for himself on a tour through North America by inviting scientists to watch and film his performance. Geller claimed he was not an ordinary magician with skilled deceptive hands, but someone who was genuinely in touch with powerful unknown forces. He was particularly adept at bending silverware and starting stopped watches. (First question: Someone who's got genuine super-powers shows off by… *bending silverware*?)

After baffling a number of genuine scientists, and getting quite a bit of press for it, Geller was eventually unmasked by other magicians who felt he was giving the magic community a bad name. Plus, they kept pointing out, he's not even very good. What baffles us, they would say, is not the bent silverware. It's the fact that he's getting away with it.

Having seen the videos, we would argue that Geller's technique was in fact excellent. It's true that his hands are not as good as many others (see Ricky Jay videos for incredible hands) but his tongue and manner were terrific. What follows is a description of a bent silverware trick which beautifully illustrates the single most important "trick" in a magician's bag: misdirection. A good magician keeps the audience's attention where he wants it, not where it should be. Here is how it goes.

THE FAMOUS PSYCHO BENT SPOON EXPERIMENT. The psychic sits down in a laboratory viewing room at a table full of lab coated scientists, surrounded on all sides. He is not wearing long sleeves or a jacket. The room, table, and chairs are completely new to him. All the spectators are from the laboratory. There is no chance any of them are in cahoots. A metal-detecting wand is used to establish that he has no

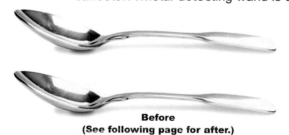

metal anywhere upon his body. A video camera is trained on him at all times.

Two spoons are brought into the room. He has never seen them before and they are provided by the lab. He does

Before
(See following page for after.)

not touch them but asks that they be inspected to ensure the fact that they are identical. All examine them and all agree: identical. The man has kept his hands in full view and never touches the spoons.

The two are set in front of him and the psychic asks which would the viewers like to see him bend. They indicate one and the man explains that he is not always able to bend the metal and that in many cases the change is very subtle. "Hence," he says, "this second spoon, which we will call the 'control spoon.' We will use it for comparison." He puts it aside. "If I am successful, we will compare the two and see."

For the next 20 minutes the psychic speaks quietly and concentrates intensely on the test spoon which sits directly in front of him. Although he moves his hands over it very frequently, everybody is watching carefully. He never touches it. Afterwards, the video is reviewed and the same conclusion is reached. He gets close, but at no time does he actually touch the spoon.

Eventually, he leans back. He is sweaty and obviously exhausted. "I do not think I have been successful. It has been very difficult. So many people here are doubters. But still, there is always a chance. Let others do the comparison." He gets up from his chair and stands back.

A hushed silence ensues. The two spoons are brought together and after a careful examination, a growing exclamation is heard and

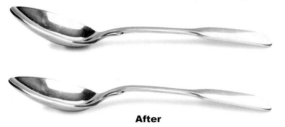

After

a startling conclusion is reached. There is a small, but perceptible difference. Impossible. Everybody is absolutely positive, he never touched the spoon!

And, of course, he didn't. He didn't have to since he bent the comparison spoon as he put it aside. But no one was watching that since all eyes were on the spoon that sat in front of him.

If you watch the video again keeping an eye on the move, you'll see it quite clearly, although he's definitely quick about it. Every magician who watches sees it instantly but scientists in particular have their eyes riveted on the spoon they're supposed to.

If you like magic and like being entertained, watch this hand.

A PORTRAIT IN MISDIRECTION

If your thing is busting magicians, watch this one.

It's a beautiful piece of magic because misdirection and presentation aren't just a big part of it, they are all of it. Bending a spoon as you put it down on the table does not take years of practice, but you can fool a lab full of scientists if you know how to manipulate their attention. And while the whole show takes 20 minutes, the dirty work is done in the first few seconds. A true classic.

What follows is a small piece of insta-magic that relies on the same principle, along with the power of suggestion. We include it here to illustrate the same point: misdirection is the secret.

THE NO-PRACTICE COIN VANISH.

Reach into your pocket and pull out a coin.

Rub it against your arm as shown. Explain that you are trying to rub off the copper coating. (This is a lie. You're actually making them watch your moving hand.)

Fake drop the coin a couple of times. Keep talking during the drops and *pick them up with your other, non-rubbing hand*. Don't look at the pick-up, look at your audience.

After each pick-up, switch hands with the coin and go back to rubbing.

**Start here.
One quarter.**

**Rest your chin, and
pick up the quarter.**

Rub on arm.

**...and give it back to
your rubbing hand.**

Go back to rubbing.

**Drop it again.
You're really clumsy.**

On the third drop, do everything exactly as before only this time, fake the hand-off. Keep the coin in your non-rubbing hand but pretend that you got it. It's not hard and since no one is looking anyway, it hardly matters how badly you do it.

Go back to rubbing. But since this time you don't have a coin in the rubbing hand, you're faking the whole thing. Eventually (and slowly) stop rubbing and reveal that the coin has been rubbed entirely through the skin and has now completely vanished. While everyone is astonished at that, just drop the real coin down your shirt collar.

Keep rubbing.

Whoops. Dropped it.

Pick it up with your chin hand...

Pick up with chin hand.

Fake this pass. It's super easy. Keep the coin in the chin hand.

Done. The rubbing hand is empty. Drop the coin in collar.

Learning how to be a magician is really learning how to work your audience. You need to make every trick a big story. It's like telling a joke. Build the tension, sharpen the timing, and keep their eyes where you want them. You can make some very bad jokes hysterical with good presentation, and you can make some lame tricks amazing the same way.

In other words, it's not about the trick, it's all about the

How to Make Sharpie® Shoes

You will need: some Sharpie pens of different colors and a pair of white tennies. Some people like to practice on a piece of paper beforehand just to work out the design. Or you can just wing it. In either case, you'll end up with shoes you can't buy at any store.

And other low-cost video special effects

How to Knock Off a Head

The people in movies live much more exciting lives than you do. They're always getting thrown into the air by the blast of exploding fuel trucks. Or they talk to animals or fly though the air or spin their heads around while lots of slow-motion hot lead just barely misses them. And then they go to a fancy party filled with beautiful women and evil scientists.

It's frustrating. And it probably makes you feel pretty darn ordinary.

But here's a way to fight back. Fake it. Shoot video that makes it look like you're doing all that stuff. To be honest, we think some of the movies fake it, too.

All you need is some kind of video camera. Doesn't matter if it's just a cheapie drugstore kind or what. Even a point-and-shoot still camera with a video feature works. You can replace a lot of equipment with a little imagination. These are all little one-act plays that we would like to see. If you shoot one, please post it and let us know where. We'd love to see it.

Shoot. Hit pause. Sister leaves.   **Shoot. Hit pause.**   **Replace with dog.**

Turn Your Sister Into a Dog. The single most basic video trick of all goes like this: Shoot, freeze, and stop. Swap something out, and then start shooting again. It's the very oldest special effect of all. Here we swap a sister for a dog, but you can change brothers into frogs, pickles into penguins, people into potholders, etc. Or, if you like, just make things vanish.

Knock Off His Head. Get your friend to sit on the back of a couch facing away from you. Then make them hang their head so their chin is on their chest. Lastly, balance a grocery bag on their shoulders as if it were over their head. Turn the camera on and make them say things like, "Hey! Can I take this stupid bag off my head? I don't get the joke." While they're doing that, get a huge pillow, tiptoe up to them, and then whack the bag so it goes flying off. Shoot it from the front and it'll look like you knocked their head completely off. Very cool.

swing!

I Am a Hot Dog. Put your camera on a table right in front of you and pointed at your face. Turn it on and smile. Then, pick it up and bring it slowly to your open mouth so that everything goes… black. Keep a finger over the lens and start making all kinds of munching and digestive groaning sounds. After you've shaken it and gurgled for a while, put it in the bottom of a (dry) bathroom sink and hit the toilet handle while you take your finger off the lens. Spin the camera with the sound of flushing in the background. Cut to black. Makes a great little science film.

Fighting Phones. You'll need a friend or two, each with a cell phone. The basic idea is to make phones into talking puppets (sort of) that don't like each other, that start insulting each other, and eventually start punching each other out. It's the old familiar story of an ancient stupid pointless feud. Here is how to shoot it.

Shoot from the side.   **Cut.**   **Then take turns shooting each phone like this.**

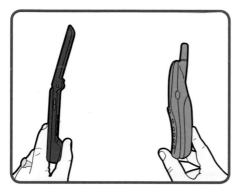

Phone P.O.V.

Put a cell phone in each hand and get a couple of friends to call each of them. (Come to think of it, they don't even have to be there.) Put the phones both on speaker and while you're shooting everything as if it were a puppet show, let the insults begin.

Your friends can take turns hollering at each other. If you get tired of shooting everything from the side, switch it up and shoot each phone directly, one at a time, as it insults "you." (It's like in the movies when the camera takes the point of view of one of the fighters.)

Eventually, bring the two cameras together so they can duke it out. When one of them wins, it should strut around and make a big deal of it. Cut to black.

IF YOU REALLY LIKED THESE ACTIVITIES Check out our title *Tricky Video*, and check out the videos themselves at klutz.com/tv.

This Is Your Lucky Page

THIS SIDE UP

Cut out. Place in wallet.

With so many systems in place to guarantee good luck and grant wishes these days, it's hard to know which one will really work the best for you.

That's why we've decided to improve your odds (rim shot) and include seven on these two pages. If you do all the following, it's hard to see how things can go anyway but right for you for pretty much the rest of your life. Give it about 20 years and then give us a call to tell us how it went.

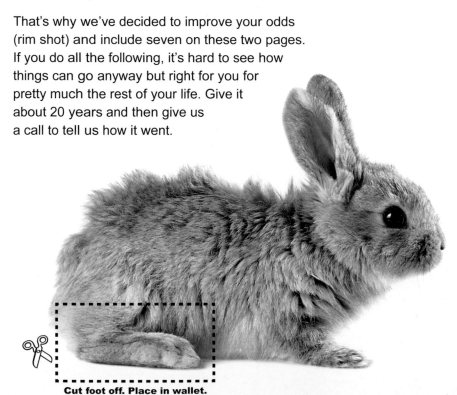

Cut foot off. Place in wallet.

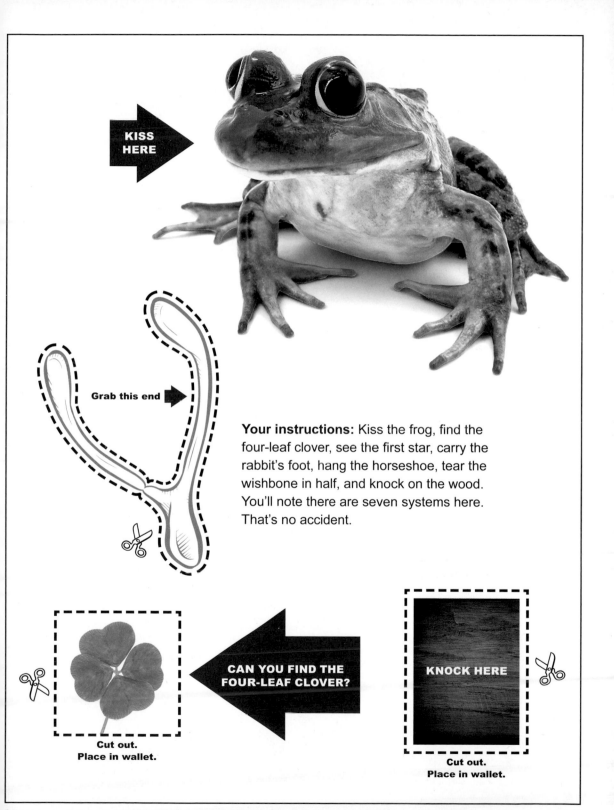

KISS HERE

Grab this end

Your instructions: Kiss the frog, find the four-leaf clover, see the first star, carry the rabbit's foot, hang the horseshoe, tear the wishbone in half, and knock on the wood. You'll note there are seven systems here. That's no accident.

CAN YOU FIND THE FOUR-LEAF CLOVER?

KNOCK HERE

Cut out.
Place in wallet.

Cut out.
Place in wallet.

Bobbing for Strawberries

We don't include a lot of party games because, quite frankly, most of them are quite lame. Mother May I? Pin the Tail on the Donkey? *Please*.

There are, however, a rare few exceptions… like this one.

The rules are not complicated. Fill a big mixing bowl with whipped cream and place a strawberry somewhere in the middle of it. Then, contestants have to get the strawberry out and eat it. Best time wins.

Simple.

Oh. And did we mention you can't use your hands?

How to Play Nose Bonk

We believe the simplest games are often the best. And it's hard to get much simpler than Nose Bonk. Here's how it goes:

Lay down on the ground with your heads together. Throw the sock up in the air so it lands on somebody else's nose. Or at least tries to. No fair catching it! That's it. Any questions?

How to Balance a Ping-Pong Ball on Your Nose

Although this looks extremely difficult, it's actually quite easy. All you need to do is cheat.

1 Before anyone is looking put a small piece of clear cellophane tape on the ping-pong ball.Fold it into a little loop so that it's sticky on both sides.

2 Go find a crowd, the bigger the better. Make a big noisy deal about how you're going to balance a ping-pong ball on your nose.They will not believe you. So…

3 Throw your head back, carefully place the ping-pong ball on your nose (so it sticks), and then stagger around the room knocking over chairs and stuff.

The magic of cellophane tape

Blindfolded Makeovers

Another sleepover special. If you're the one getting the makeover, be sure to put cucumbers over your eyes before it all starts. For two reasons. One, you'll get that marvelous refreshed vegetabley feeling, and two, the other kid can't poke your eye out.

Beyond that, the instructions are pretty much contained in the picture. By the way, some mothers are more open to this than others, especially since it's probably going to be their make-up. You might want to check beforehand.

And be sure to take turns.

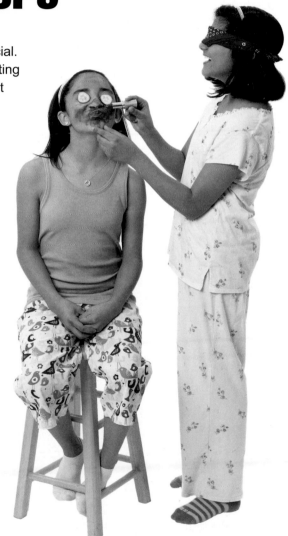

The World's Greatest No-Practice Card Trick

A lot of card tricks are pretty easy, some are quite easy, but only a very few are brain-dead easy. And then beyond that, how many of them are any good?

Only one. Here it is.

❶ Cut the five pieces of card out very carefully. Stay exactly on the gray lines. If you have a paper cutter, use it. The King looks nice with his beard and long hair. Count the pieces again — five, right?

❷ Now turn all the pieces over and assemble the back of the card, the circles with border pattern. Count the pieces again. Notice anything funny?

❸ That's right! You have an extra piece that you don't need to complete the back side of the card. Have your audience try to explain why the King needs five pieces to come together when he's facing you, and only four pieces when he's not.

Repeat as often as you like. It works every time, even the first.
One side comes together with a piece missing, one side does not.
True no-practice magic.

PS: Incidentally, it's not at all clear to us how this trick works. We just know it does. If you can figure it out, drop us a line.

194

Set a world record

How to Stand Out in a Crowd of 7 Billion

We all know the problem. With today's growing world population, it's becoming harder and harder to get enough notice. Fortunately, we have here a stern but simple solution: Be a World Record Holder! Take on one challenge — one mountain — and climb it higher than anyone else before you, until you and you alone stand atop it, gazing over a massive crowd of 7 billion lessers.

But where are these unconquered mountains? Here is one, perhaps the most prominent of all…

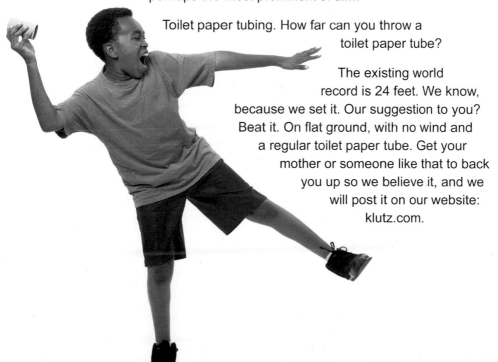

Toilet paper tubing. How far can you throw a toilet paper tube?

The existing world record is 24 feet. We know, because we set it. Our suggestion to you? Beat it. On flat ground, with no wind and a regular toilet paper tube. Get your mother or someone like that to back you up so we believe it, and we will post it on our website: klutz.com.

Answers

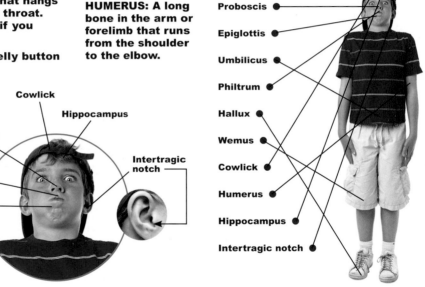

PAGE 18

Name That Body Part

PROBOSCIS: Nose

EPIGLOTTIS: The lid-like flap of elastic cartilage tissue covered with a mucous membrane, attached to the root of the tongue. In other words, it's that little doomaflachie that hangs down into your throat. You can see it if you open wide.

UMBILICUS: Belly button

PHILTRUM: The midline groove in the upper lip that runs from the top of the lip to the nose

HALLUX: Big toe

WEMUS: the skin located on the top of your knee.

HIPPOCAMPUS: The front part of your brain. You have two. Or at least you're supposed to.

HUMERUS: A long bone in the arm or forelimb that runs from the shoulder to the elbow.

COWLICK: A cowlick appears when the growth direction of the hair forms a spiral pattern.

INTERTRAGIC NOTCH: The deep notch in the lower part of the auricle (the principal projecting part of the ear) between the tragus and antitragus.

Cowlick
Hippocampus
Proboscis
Philtrum
Epiglottis
Intertragic notch

Proboscis •
Epiglottis •
Umbilicus •
Philtrum •
Hallux •
Wemus •
Cowlick •
Humerus •
Hippocampus •
Intertragic notch •

PAGE 135

Talk Like a Pirate

❶ Avast or Belay = Cut that out! (E)

❷ Ahoy = Howdy (F)

❸ Scuttle = Call off (I)

❹ Bucko = Good Pal (J)

❺ Abaft = Behind (A)

❻ Booty = Loot (D)

❼ Smart = Quickly (L)

❽ Aloft = Up above (M)

❾ Lubber = One who lives on land (C)

❿ Beauty = Girl (K)

⓫ Weigh anchor or cast off = leave (N)

⓬ Aye = Yes (B)

⓭ Matey = Guy you've just met (H)

⓮ Me = My (G)

Acknowledgments

Editor
John Cassidy

Design
Kevin Plottner

Illustration
Buc Rogers

Photography
Peter Fox
Rebekah Lovato
Liz Hutnick

Editorial Assistance
Rebekah Lovato
Deja Delaney
Pat Murphy

Production
Mimi Oey

Help
Marybeth Arago
David Barker
Chris Barry
John Baur
Kevin Beales
Nicholas Berger
Paul Chaiken
John Collins
Steve Diamond
Nathan Diehl
Paul Doherty
Sam Freeman
Patrick House
Liz Hutnick
Theresa Hutnick
Johan Lehrer
Marty Magneson
Barb Magnus
Gary Mcdonald
Josh Mulholland
Jenna Nybank
Bill Olson
Lisa Plisco
Jeff Raz
Alan Robbins
Eva Steele-Saccio
Robert D. San Souci
Mark Summers
Elliot Tomlinson
 and his friend Sam
Laura Torres
Liebe Wetzel
Valerie Wyatt

Models
Andre P. Augustin Jr., Tiffani
Baker, Patrick Barry, Tessa
Barry, Aidan Berger, Nicholas
Berger, Isabelle Blanchard,
Tatiana Boyle, Dylan Chandley,
Thomas Christenson, The
Chu Family, Ethan Davis, Isis
Decrem, Nathan Diehl, Manar
Eldeen, Bo Field, Graham
Fisher, Jenner Fox, Kaela Fox,
Franz, Katie Garvey, Lauren
Geiselhart, Alfredo G. Gonzalez,
Gabriel Greening, Jeff Harrison,
Wade Hauser, Hayden, Virgilio
Hernandez, Sean Hinton,
Tasuku Hirakawa, Katrina
Hough, Eric Jensen, Linda
Jensen, Anand Joshi, Richard
Kramer, Sophia Krugler, Sithara
Kumar, Julia Kwasnick,
Karen Kuo,

The Lawson Family,
Ryan J. Leong, Sarah
Limb, Lexie Livingston,
Rebekah Lovato, Leigh
Mercer, Aylin Montes,
Bill Olsen, Matt O'Reilly,
Lucy Oyer, Gopika Prabhu,
Jaxon Rafanan-Seer, Marion M.
Rehbock, Jack Robinson, Zack
Ross, Avi Sachs, Jon Samos,
Noel Sanborn, Julia Sanchez,
Brandon Schneider, Lennon
Seiders, Tyler Simons, Robert
Smith, Mukund Sreenivasan,
Raj Sreenivasan, Ashvin
Srinivasan, Raz Steinhart,
Yuvan Steinhart, Chipper Stotz,
Madeline TA, Julie Toennis,
Emily Ting, Hannah Tumminaro,
Holly Tumminaro, Jill Turney,
Blake Vesey, Christopher Viola,
Hans VonClemm, Nicholas
Welch, Bud "Claude" Weaver,
Eric Wesoff, Lauren Zenger,
Mitch Zenger, The Zenger
Family, Peter Ziebelman

Credits
Cover: Art derived from
AMERICAN GOTHIC, 1930, by
Grant Wood. All rights reserved
by the Estate of Nan Wood
Graham/Licensed by VAGA,
New York, NY. Page 12:
Leaves © iStockphoto.com/
fotosav. Page 13: Bottle ©
iStockphoto.com/Tjanze.
Page 24: Toilet ©
iStockphoto.com/
Creativel.
Pages 32–33:
Dimes

© iStockphoto.
com/clickstock
and © iStockphoto.
com/TokenPhoto.
Pages 40–41: Frames
© iStockphoto.com/
sub, © iStockphoto.
com/LastSax and ©
iStockphoto.com/gbrundin.
Page 44: Hearts © iStockphoto.
com/song_mi. Page 52:
Homework © fotokate - Fotolia.
com. Page 52: Note paper ©
iStockphoto.com/muratsen.
Page 57: Chimp © iStockphoto.
com/kiamsoon. Page 67:
Football field © iStockphoto.
com/cscredon; Cardboard ©
iStockphoto.com/billnoll;
Pill bug © iStockphoto.com/
jeffhochstrasser; Cow
© iStockphoto.com/narvikk
Page 69: Pool © iStockphoto.
com/LordRunar.

What came before Volume 2?

How to Never Grow Up Again

Volume 1

Being one of our alert readers, you will have noticed that this book is entitled *The Encyclopedia of Immaturity: Volume 2.* And in your restless mind this will raise a question: Volume 2? Does that mean... ?

Yes, gentle reader, there is a *Volume 1.* Filled with 400 pages of almost exactly the same material except entirely different. Subtitled *How to Never Grow Up: The Complete Guide,* it is filled with precisely the same sort of activities, skills, mischief, and, of course, secret knowledge. The material was collected by John Cassidy over a completely misspent lifetime of immaturity and irresponsibility and as a result, there is no other book quite like it. Except one. Which you've already got.

Volume 2

The Outtakes

A great many things that we prepared for this book were cut as the editing process went on. Here are a few.

Be a Human Cannonball

How to Sit on Flagpoles

Ice Cream Taster, Sword Swallower and Other Career Choices

How to Charm Snakes

How to Procrastinate: A Guide for Busy People

How to Lose at Spin the Bottle

How to Build a Fly-Powered Paper Airplane

How to Make Cool Snares and Pitfalls

How to Break Bricks with Your Forehead

Snowball Fights: Winning Strategies

How to Slide Down Banisters (And Still Have Kids)

Cardboard Sledding: A Guide to Hillside Terror

How to Hypnotize Teachers

How to Dodge Sloppy Aunt Kisses

How to Leave a False Trail

Is This Edible? The Complete Concoction Cookbook

It's Just Not Fair: The Pluto Petition

How to Catch and Train Lightning Bugs